Running

Chamonix
and the
Mont Blanc
region

About the Author

Kingsley's love of the mountains started as a five-year-old. It wasn't a big surprise that he studied geography and glaciology at university. He's climbed the north faces of the Eiger, Matterhorn and Grandes Jorasses in the Alps, and led expeditions to mountains all over the world. Through mountaineering he developed a passion for a minimalist approach in the mountains, and soon discovered trail running as an ultimate form of fast and light travel.

Over the years Kingsley has participated in many mountain ultra running events, including the Tor des Geants and five finishes (and counting) of Ultra Trail du Mont Blanc series races (two UTMBs, two TDSs and one CCC), as well as many mountain races including the Chamonix Marathon, 80km du Mont Blanc, Zermatt Marathon, Lakes in a Day, and countless others. He's also run in Vertical Kilometer races in the Alps and fell races in the UK.

He runs a mountain running and guiding company (www.icicle.co.uk), and so divides his time between the Alps and the Lake District each year. This peripatetic lifestyle enables him to guide running groups in the mountains throughout the year, and his qualifications range from UIMLA International Mountain Leader to Personal Trainer. While researching all the routes in this book, Kingsley was accompanied by Maximus, his ever faithful four-legged training partner.

Twitter: @KingsleyJones
Website: www.icicle.co.uk

Trail
Running

Chamonix and the Mont Blanc region

**40 routes
in the Chamonix Valley,
Italy and Switzerland**

by Kingsley Jones

2 Police Square, Milnthorpe
Cumbria LA7 7PY

www.cicerone.co.uk

Printed in China on behalf of Latitude Press Ltd

A catalogue record for this book is available from the British Library.

Route mapping
by Lovell Johns
www.lovelljohns.com

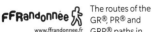

The routes of the GR®, PR® and GRP® paths in this guide have been reproduced with the permission of the Fédération Française de la Randonnée Pédestre holder of the exclusive rights of the routes. The names GR®, PR® and GRP® are registered trademarks. © FFRP 2016 for all GR®, PR® and GRP® paths appearing in this work.

The trademarks Ultra-Trail®, UTMB®, Ultra-Trail du Mont Blanc®, CCC®, TDS®, PTL® as well as the little runner logo, are the property of Catherine Poletti, CEO Autour du Mont-Blanc s.a.r.l.

All photographs are by the author unless otherwise stated.

Contains OpenStreetMap.org data © OpenStreetMap contributors, CC-BY-SA. NASA relief data courtesy of ESRI

Acknowledgements

This book is the result of years of research and countless pairs of trail running shoes. There are too many people to thank for their input, but I'm deeply indebted to all the running clients and friends who accompanied me on the routes, and none more so than my Bernese mountain dog Maximus, who knows these trails better than anyone else. This book is dedicated to him and all those who've accompanied me on the routes described here.

A huge thanks to all the team at Cicerone for their support and belief in this project: Jonathan, Lois and Andrea, and also to Georgia for her patience in editing. Thanks to Michael and Catherine Poletti for allowing me to share their inspirational UTMB race routes. Finally, the biggest debt of gratitude is to Sarah and Freya for putting up with me doing endless route research, which those less charitable might have described as escaping the house to go on yet another run!

Updates to this Guide

While every effort is made by our authors to ensure the accuracy of guidebooks as they go to print, changes can occur during the lifetime of an edition. Any updates that we know of for this guide will be on the Cicerone website (www.cicerone.co.uk/800/updates), so please check before planning your trip. We also advise that you check information about such things as transport, accommodation and shops locally. Even rights of way can be altered over time.

The route maps in this guide are derived from publicly-available data, databases and crowd-sourced data. As such they have not been through the detailed checking procedures that would generally be applied to a published map from an official mapping agency, although naturally we have reviewed them closely in the light of local knowledge as part of the preparation of this guide.

We are always grateful for information about any discrepancies between a guidebook and the facts on the ground, sent by email to info@cicerone.co.uk or by post to Cicerone, 2 Police Square, Milnthorpe LA7 7PY, United Kingdom.

Front cover: Running on the Plan d'Aiguille above Chamonix (Route 1)

Contents

Symbols used on route maps

Symbol	Description	Relief in metres

~ route

- - - alternative route

(S) start point

(F) finish point

(SF) start/finish point

(S) alternative start

(F) alternative/finish point

glacier

woodland

urban areas

regional border

international border

—■— station/railway

▲ peak

● ● town/village

⬆ ⬆ manned/unmanned refuge

≍ bridge

■ building

□ ruin(s)

⚲ ⚲ † church/monastery/cross

)(pass

• other feature

Relief
in metres

5000 and above

4800–5000

4600–4800

4400–4600

4200–4400

4000–4200

3800–4000

3600–3800

3400–3600

3200–3400

3000–3200

2800–3000

2600–2800

2400–2600

2200–2400

2000–2200

1800–2000

1600–1800

1400–1600

1200–1400

1000–1200

800–1000

600–800

400–600

200–400

0–200

SCALE: 1:100,000

0 kilometres 1 2

0 miles 1

Contour lines are drawn at 50m intervals and highlighted at 200m intervals.

GPX files

GPX files for all routes can be downloaded free at www.cicerone.co.uk/800/GPX

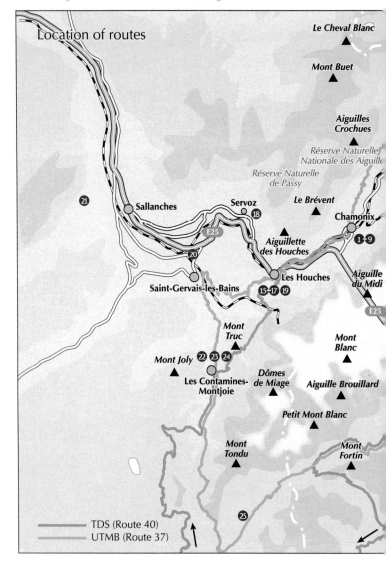

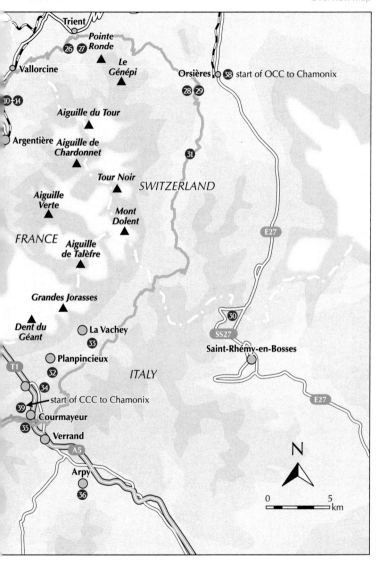

Trient

Pointe
Ronde
26 27

Vallorcine

Le
Génépi

Orsières 38 start of OCC to Chamonix

10-14

28 29

Aiguille du Tour

Argentière Aiguille de
Chardonnet

31

Tour Noir SWITZERLAND

Aiguille
Verte

Mont
Dolent

FRANCE Aiguille
de Talèfre

E27

Grandes Jorasses

Dent du
Géant

La Vachey
33

30

SS27

Saint-Rhémy-en-Bosses

Planpincieux

T1

ITALY

32

34

start of CCC to Chamonix

39

Courmayeur

35

E27

Verrand

A5

N

Arpy

36

0   5
└────────┘ km

Route summary table

Route		Grade	Distance	Ascent	Descent	Time	Page
France							
Chamonix start							
1	Mer de Glace	Trail running 2	15.3km (9½ miles)	1260m (4135ft)	1270m (4165ft)	4hr 30min	38
2	River track to Argentière	Trail running 1	8.8km (5½ miles)	221m (725ft)	10m (35ft)	1hr 20min	43
3	Merlet	Trail running 3	15.5km (9¾ miles)	710m (2330ft)	930m (3050ft)	2hr 45min	47
4	La Flégère	Trail running 2	10.8km (6¾ miles)	810m (2675ft)	610m 2000ft)	2hr 15min	53
5	Refuge Moède Anterne	Trail running 3	17.5km (11 miles)	430m (1410ft)	2100m (6890ft)	3hr 45min	57
6	La Jonction	Trail running 4	12.5km (7¾ miles)	1530m (5020ft)	1530m (5020ft)	3hr 45min	60
7	Chamonix Vertical KM	Skyrunning 4	3.8km (2½ miles)	1000m (3280ft)	0m	1hr	65
8	Marathon du Mont Blanc	Trail running 2	42km (27 miles)	2722m (8930ft)	1674m (5490ft)	7hr 15min	68
9	80km du Mont Blanc	Trail running 4	83.7km (52 miles)	6048m (19,840ft)	6048m (19,840ft)	18hrs	74
Vallorcine valley start							
10	Lac d'Emosson	Trail running 4	12km (7½ miles)	890m (2920ft)	890m (2920ft)	3hr 15min	82
11	Col de la Terrasse	Trail running 4	15.3km (9½ miles)	1380m (4525ft)	1490m (4890ft)	4hr 45min	86
12	Albert Premier	Trail running 3	15.5km (9¾ miles)	1455m (4775ft)	1305m (4280ft)	4hr 15min	90
13	Aiguilles Rouges	Trail running 3	24.5km (15¼ miles)	1410m (4625ft)	1945m (6380ft)	5hr 30min	94

Route		Grade	Distance	Ascent	Descent	Time	Page
14	Mont Buet	Trail running 4	18km (11 miles)	1775m (5825ft)	1775m (5825ft)	5hr 30min	100
Les Houches/Servoz start							
15	Le Brévent	Trail running 3	12.3km (7¾ miles)	1620m (5315ft)	125m (410ft)	4hr 15min	105
16	Le Prarion	Trail running 2	19.8km (12¼ miles)	1340m (4395ft)	1340m (4395ft)	5hrs	109
17	Col de Tricot	Trail running 3	15.5km (9¾ miles)	1400m (4595ft)	1245m (4085ft)	4hr 15min	114
18	Lac Vert	Trail running 1	12.6km (7¾ miles)	560m (1835ft)	775m (2540ft)	2hr 45min	118
19	Charousse	Trail running 1	8km (5 miles)	330m (1080ft)	520m (1705ft)	1hr 30min	122
Sallanches/St Gervais/Les Contamines start							
20	Nid d'Aigle	Trail running 3	20.4km (12¾ miles)	1695m (5560ft)	100m (330ft)	3hr 30min	125
21	Refuge de Doran	Trail running 2	11.9km (7½ miles)	995m (3265ft)	995m (3265ft)	3hrs	129
22	Mont Truc	Trail running 1	12.8km (8 miles)	805m (2640ft)	805m (2640ft)	2hr 30min	133
23	Mont Joly	Trail running 3	19.4km (12 miles)	1405m (4690ft)	1405m (4690ft)	4hr 30min	136
24	Refuge de Tré-le-Tête	Trail running 3	13.7km (8½ miles)	1005m (3300ft)	1005m (3300ft)	3hr 15min	140
Les Chapieux start							
25	Tête Nord des Fours	Trail running 3	16.1km (10 miles)	1175m (3855ft)	1175m (3855ft)	4hrs	144
Switzerland							
26	Mont de l'Arpille	Trail running 2	15.5km (9¾ miles)	770m (2525ft)	1610m (5280ft)	3hr 15min	150
27	Croix de Fer	Trail running 3	16.6km (10¼ miles)	1135m (3725ft)	1135m (3725ft)	4hrs	154

On the marathon track to Vallorcine (Route 8)

The Aiguille Noire from the TDS race route (Route 40)

Introduction

The boundaries between mountain sports are blurring, largely driven by the development of better clothing, equipment and training. Most noticeably there is a greater desire for people to travel further, faster and lighter than ever before. Trail running is the embodiment of this movement, driven by simplicity and the joy of pushing one's limits in glorious scenery. Trail running gives us freedom.

As humans we are born runners. Our Neolithic forefathers were persistence hunters, using a combination of running and tracking to pursue prey until it was exhausted. Nowadays we see the effects of modern diet and work environments having a detrimental impact on many people's health. The attraction of running is that it's a sport that comes naturally to us; it requires very little equipment, improves our health and hugely benefits us mentally too.

There's a natural progression for those who run to seek the next challenge – be it in terms of distance or on tougher terrain – and the mountains provide the most extreme medium in which to practise our sport. At the pinnacle of this, elite runners have run up famous Alpine peaks including Mont Blanc and the Matterhorn, at fantastic speeds compared to the rest of us mortals.

One of the main draws of trail running is that you move fast and unencumbered, compared to the average trekker or climber, and that opens up new horizons in what you can achieve. Mountain running brings a sense of liberation that it is rarely felt – even while walking or mountaineering.

Given the sport's increased popularity, gone are the preconceptions of mountain runners as wild mountain men with overly short shorts and wild beards. You're more likely to be overtaken by a woman in the latest technical compression fabrics with lightweight poles and a minimalist running backpack. Trail running has come a long way in the last 20 years; it's more inclusive, more accessible, and more enjoyable than ever before.

In the Chamonix Mont Blanc region, trail running is a way of life. The big ultra trails are the beating heart of the sporting calendar in many of its villages. There's great support from the locals at these events – even if it means getting up in the middle of the night to cheer runners passing through, or to help at the aid stations. There's a palpable buzz in the valleys when a trail race is on. All ages get swept along with the excitement, from the old farmer ringing a cow bell to young children standing beside the trail with their tiny hands outstretched to clap those of passing runners.

Trail running is far more than a selfish personal quest; it's a sport that brings people together, shares a love of the mountains, and inspires

Relief on finishing the Ultra Trail du Mont Blanc (Route 37)

others. The aim of this book, and of the routes described, is to help motivate you to enjoy this thrilling sport in one of its greatest playgrounds. While goals such as pace, time and terrain will differ from runner to runner, the shared goal should be the pursuit of maximum enjoyment with the minimum of equipment or impact on the landscape.

This book will introduce you to the world of trail running on some of the finest trails in the Alps, around all corners of the Mont Blanc massif – a mecca for trail runners and the venue for some of the greatest trail running races in the world, such as the Tor des Géants and Ultra Trail du Mont Blanc. The routes selected in this guide are of specific interest for runners in terms of the terrain they cover, the distances

travelled, or the vertical height gains encountered.

The intention is to share with the reader some of the best locations for trail running around the Mont Blanc massif, as well as providing a brief grounding in the safety aspects, training and equipment to consider. The key focus has been to keep this book as portable and condensed as possible, to ensure that it always earns a space in your running bag. It's outside the scope of this book to provide a comprehensive manual about trail running, but the information given in the introduction, as well as the individual tips included within the routes, will give you some great ideas to try out, while the focus is on showing you the best places to run.

THE CHAMONIX MONT BLANC REGION

As you drive up the Autoroute Blanche from Geneva to Chamonix your spirits lift at the sight of the bright glistening peaks of the Mont Blanc massif ahead, which straddles the borders of France, Italy, and Switzerland. Mont Blanc is the highest point at just over 4800m.

All the northern and western aspects of the range are in France, the southern aspect is Italian, and the eastern aspect is Swiss. Over time the borders have fluctuated – most recently with the former Kingdom of Savoie being split and annexed into parts of the Aosta region of Italy and the French Republic, just over 150 years ago.

There is still ongoing uncertainty over the exact border in places – a famed example being the Mont Blanc summit shown as being shared by France and Italy on Italian maps, whereas on French maps the border line veers further south, so all the summit is shown as completely in France. Despite these historical differences, what unifies the region are its mountains.

On all aspects, the mountain range was seen as a poor upland area before the massive growth in tourism brought huge changes and wealth to the region. Mont Blanc was first climbed in 1786 by Balmat and Paccard, but mountaineering really started with the golden age of alpinism in the 1860s, which saw climbers including Edward Whymper making key first ascents in the massif.

Running towards Refuge de Loriaz (Route 10)

A runner framed by the distinctive profile of Les Drus (Route 1)

Tourism started slowly, with visitors marvelling at the Mer de Glace at Montenvers in the 18th century, having ascended on foot or by mule. A key milestone was when Chamonix hosted the first ever Winter Olympics in 1924, after which it grew famous as an Alpine capital for winter sports. The Second World War saw occupations on either side of the massif, with the highest battle of the war fought across the Col du Midi.

In the last 50 years tourism has grown rapidly on all sides of the massif, and sporting events ranging from the Kandahar Ski World Cup to the Piolets d'Or climbing awards are hosted locally each year, confirming the reputation of the area as a mecca for extreme sports. More recently, world-class trail running events have been established, including the Ultra Trail du Mont Blanc (UTMB) and the Tor des Géants. These are huge dates on the local and international sporting calendar.

You'd be forgiven for thinking that the winter season must be busier for tourist numbers, due to the size of the ski industry, but in recent years there have actually been more summer visitors for walking, climbing, paragliding, mountain biking and sightseeing. One of the key areas of growth has been in numbers of trail runners: accommodation on key race weeks, such as the Chamonix Marathon or UTMB is scarcer than it is over New Year. Trail running has arrived on a massive scale, and is now crucial to the local economy.

Bases for a trail running holiday

There's a wide range of accommodation available in the Mont Blanc region – and Chamonix in particular – which may be of interest to runners. This varies from some excellent campsites to chalets and five-star hotels, so there's something for every budget and taste.

The Chamonix valley in France, to the north of the Mont Blanc massif, is the key region for tourism. If you're looking for a base for your holiday, this is the most convenient, but if you want to avoid the busy town centre you could look at staying in quieter villages along the train line up the valley, such as Vallorcine or Argentière. To the west of the massif, the Les Contamines valley in France is a great base too, and you'd escape the tourists a bit more there.

Italy is generally cheaper to stay in, and the food's great. Options include the main town of Courmayeur or the village of Pré Saint Didier just down the valley. The south side of Mont Blanc is famed for being the sunny side, and if you like good coffee and ice cream it's the place to be.

The eastern aspect is Swiss, and much less developed, with the only main tourist town being Champex. If you want to base yourself in Switzerland, Martigny is practical as a transport hub, although Champex is quieter and far prettier.

The Chamonix Mont Blanc region caters well for campers and there's no shortage of attractive, well-equipped sites. In the Chamonix valley the campsites of Mer de Glace in Les Praz (www.chamonix-camping.com), Camping du Glacier d'Argentière in Chosalets (www.campingchamonix. com) and l'île des Barrats in Chamonix (www.campingdesbarrats.com) are all popular bases. Les Praz has the most pitches in the shade of trees, so runners don't return to a tent that feels like an oven after a hard day on the trails. On the Italian side, the best campsite is Les Grandes Jorasses in the Val Ferret (www.grandesjorasses. com/en/), while in Switzerland the Les Rocailles in Champex (champex-camping.ch) is recommended.

For those who prefer a roof over their heads, at the cheaper end of the scale there are youth hostels and cheap rooms available in all of the valleys surrounding the Mont Blanc massif, such as Le Vagabond (www.gitevagabond.com) and Ski Station (www.skistation.fr), both in Chamonix. See also www.hostelworld. com. Mid-and top-range hotels can also be found throughout the area; a good place to start searching is www. booking.com. The tourist offices in Chamonix (www.chamonix.com) and Courmayeur (www.lovecourmayeur. com) offer a room finder service, which is great for making last-minute plans, as hotels often list late deals to fill rooms.

Booking ahead is always recommended – especially in the peak summer season from mid July to the end of August. Key peaks in tourist numbers are around the last weekend in June for the Chamonix Marathon weekend events; the Bastille Day celebrations, which coincide with the climbing world cup competition in Chamonix in mid July; and the last week of August, which is when the UTMB events are underway. For those seeking a quieter time, mid to late June and September are far less busy: you'll have more accommodation options and you might also have the trails to yourself.

See Appendix A for a list of useful contacts including accommodation resources and providers.

Travelling to the Alps

By air

The closest international airport to the Mont Blanc massif is Geneva, just across the Swiss border. It's well served by direct flights from all over Europe, including the UK and Ireland, both on national and budget carriers. The summer schedules are now as busy as the winter season. To search for flights, try www.skyscanner.net.

There are many airport transfer companies operating between Geneva to Chamonix. See Appendix A for transport operator contact details.

By rail

The closest high-speed train line station to the Mont Blanc massif is Saint Gervais Le Fayet, which has services that connect via Lyon to Paris. From Saint Gervais, the Mont Blanc Express train goes directly to Chamonix. If travelling from the UK, there's a new Eurostar (www.eurostar.com) service from London St Pancras through to Geneva via the Channel Tunnel and Lille.

By bus

There's a regular Eurolines (www.eurolines.co.uk) coach service from London Victoria to Chamonix. For those flying to Geneva airport, there's a regular coach and scheduled EasyBus (www.easybus.com) shuttle service to Chamonix Sud, as well as a range of private taxi companies. See Appendix A for further details.

By car

Driving to the Mont Blanc massif is very easy on the French toll road network. For those travelling from the UK, it takes approximately 8 hours to get from Calais to Chamonix. Consider breaking the journey by staying in reasonably priced budget hotels such as Formule 1 (www.hotelf1.com).

Travelling around the Chamonix valley and region

All of the routes in this guidebook are accessible by public transport, which serves the region reliably. In addition, every accommodation provider between Servoz and Vallorcine in the Chamonix valley includes a tourist tax in their price: this small levy of around €1 per day entitles guests to a *Carte d'Hôte* (Tourist Card), which enables free bus and train travel between Servoz and Vallorcine. This is a great environmental initiative, and is handy for several of the runs in this guide, where you start and finish in different locations. See Appendix A for contact details.

By rail

The Mont Blanc Express line runs the length of the Chamonix valley, its trains serving the villages in the French region as they shuttle to and fro between St Gervais Le Fayet in France and Martigny in Switzerland (www.mont-blanc-express.com). From both of these stations there are good bus services to the Swiss and French valleys and villages nearby.

In addition there is the Mont Blanc Tramway, which is operated as part of the cable car company network of mountain uplift. Its line runs from the valley at Le Fayet, all the way to the terminus at Nid d'Aigle. It's also possible to join the tramway near the Bellevue cable car station above Les Houches. Its schedule is available at www.compagniedumontblanc.fr.

By bus

From outside Chamonix train station there's a SAVDA bus to Courmayeur in Italy, and the same company provides local connections from Courmayeur bus station (www.savda.it). In addition, Le Fayet has the SAT bus service to Les Contamines (www.sat-montblanc.com) and Martigny has a regular post bus service to Champex (www.sbb.ch/en/home).

Tramway du Mont Blanc at Nid d'Aigle (Route 20)

By taxi

Taxis in the region are prohibitively expensive, and are often unavailable outside normal working hours, although many of the airport transport companies can arrange cost-effective shuttles for groups. See Appendix A for further details.

Weather and forecasts

The presence of the mountains has a far greater influence on the weather than runners may be used to – especially those from the UK. The summit of Mont Blanc, at just over 4800m, towers nearly four kilometres above the valley, and even in mid-summer the temperatures on its summit are on average -15°C. While none of the routes in this book reach the summit, many venture high on the slopes to around 3000m, where glacial katabatic (downslope) winds, foehn effects and convection storms may be severe.

The first thing a runner should do each day is check the weather forecast (chamonix-meteo.com or www.meteofrance.com) to identify any highlighted risks such as afternoon storms or a low freezing level that could result in ice on some of the trails. As ever, the runner needs to adapt their choice of route, as well as the equipment they plan to carry, to the prevailing weather.

Be aware of lenticular (lens-shaped) cloud over the Mont Blanc summit, as this indicates a humid south-westerly airstream that's likely to bring heavy precipitation within the course of a day. Northerly slopes are in the shade in the morning and have cooler katabatic winds descending their flanks, accentuated near steep north faces or glacier basins. Conversely, southerly slopes are more heated by the sun and have warm anabatic thermals rising up them. While this might sound pleasant to a runner, the rising convection cells often generate violent mid- to late-afternoon storms, so watch out for clouds bubbling up and condensing on southerly slopes.

Maps

A 1:100,000-scale map of each route is provided with the route description, but runners should always carry a separate sheet map of the area in which they're running.

The maps covering the Mont Blanc massif are provided by the French IGN (Institut National de l'Information Géographique), the Italian IGC (Istituto Geografico Centrale) and the Swiss Federal Office of Topography (swisstopo). These vary in detail, with the swisstopo being the most detailed for running – especially their 1:25,000-scale maps. For the Chamonix area IGN have distilled their sheet maps into highly compact, pocket-sized maps that are ideal for runners.

The relevant sheet maps are listed at the start of each route description, and all the maps you'll need are readily available on the internet from retailers such as Stanfords (www.stanfords.co.uk), the Map Shop www.themapshop.co.uk and Icicle (www.icicle-mountaineering.ltd.uk).

Safety and mountain rescue

Always carry the safety equipment outlined in the checklist below (see Trail kit). In the event of an accident you're not guaranteed a phone signal, so a good level of autonomy and experience is required for the more remote trail runs. Where you can make a call, the emergency phone numbers are 112 in France, 144 in Switzerland and 118 in Italy. You could also call the Peloton de Gendarmerie de Haute-Montagne (PGHM) Chamonix mountain rescue directly on +33 (0)450 531 689.

If you're out of phone signal and you can't move, use your whistle to blow six times in succession each minute. This is the international signal for rescue. Rescues are generally made by helicopter, so if you can move, secure all lose clothing and try and get into an open area free of obstacles, and turn your back to the prevailing wind. When a helicopter approaches, raise both arms above your head in a Y-shape to indicate you're in need of assistance.

If you're running alone, it's always worth letting people know where you're going and what time you plan to return. Many people use social media or email to enable their friends to raise an alarm if they haven't checked back in by a certain time.

Insurance

When running in the Alps it's essential that you're properly insured, as the costs in the event of an accident can be astronomical. In France, mountain rescue is operated by the PGHM and

Mountain Safety

Every mountain walk has its dangers, and those described in this guidebook are no exception. All who walk or climb in the mountains should recognise this and take responsibility for themselves and their companions along the way. The author and publisher have made every effort to ensure that the information contained in this guide was correct when it went to press, but they cannot accept responsibility for any loss, injury or inconvenience sustained by any person using this book.

International Distress Signal (emergency only)
Six blasts on a whistle (and flashes with a torch after dark) spaced evenly for one minute, followed by a minute's pause. Repeat until an answer is received. The response is three signals per minute followed by a minute's pause.

Helicopter Rescue
The following signals are used to communicate with a helicopter:

Help needed:
raise both arms
above head to
form a 'Y'

Help not needed:
raise one arm
above head, extend
other arm downward

Emergency telephone numbers
France: PGHM (Peloton de Gendarmerie de Haute Montagne):
tel 04 50 53 16 89; Emergency services: tel 112 (mobile phones)
Italy: Carabinieri: tel 0165 84 22 25; Emergency Services: tel 118
Switzerland: OCVS (Organisation Cantonale Valaisanne de Secours): tel 144

Weather reports
(If telephoning from the UK the dialling codes are:
France: 0033; *Italy:* 0039; *Switzerland:* 0041)

France: Chamonix: tel 08 92 68 02 74, **www.meteo.fr** or tel 3250
Italy: tel 0165 44 113
Switzerland: tel 162 (in French, German or Italian), **www.meteoschweiz.ch/en**

Note Mountain rescue can be very expensive – be adequately insured.

is free of charge. However, even if you had an accident in France, your European Health Insurance Card (EHIC) would not provide free hospital treatment, and some costs would have to be covered.

In addition, if you were to have a serious accident in France it's entirely possible that you could be transferred to a Swiss hospital such as Geneva, which is outside the EU, and so insurance would be essential. In both Switzerland and Italy the mountain rescue must be paid for – ideally covered by your insurance – as it's charged for by private companies or by the state. It's therefore a good idea to carry your insurance card with you when running.

Be sure to arrange insurance that will cover you for trail running in the three countries visited in this book

(France, Italy and Switzerland), for mountain rescue, medical treatment and repatriation. Most insurers don't differentiate between running and trekking, but it's worth double-checking when you take out a policy.

Popular insurance providers include the British Mountaineering Council (www.thebmc.co.uk/insurance), Snowcard (www.snowcard.co.uk) and DogTag (www.dogtag.co.uk). Bank card insurance is not likely to cover you for mountain rescue, so investigate before you put it to the test. Becoming member of the UK branch of the Austrian Alpine Club (AAC), which costs around £50 a year, entitles you to price reductions for overnight stays in CAF and CAI huts, and includes some insurance cover (though more limited than BMC or Snowcard).

Running on the Mont de la Saxe (Route 38)

MOUNTAIN RUNNING IN THE ALPS

What's different about running in the Alps?

Most fell or UK trail runners will find the length of the climbs in the Mont Blanc massif longer than what they're used to, so specific training should be undertaken before a trip to ensure that you get the most out of it. The trails of the region are also typically harder underfoot, so shoes with more cushioning and greater stability should generally be sought.

The effects of altitude will be apparent to any runner venturing above 2000m without properly acclimatising. While none of the routes outlined in this book venture significantly above 3000m, be prepared to fool the effects of altitude. A headache and extra fatigue are all a runner is likely to encounter; see Adapting to the Alps for advice on how to prepare for running at higher altitudes.

Another key difference is the mountain hut network, which offers runners shelter in inclement weather, as well as a source of refreshments. Huts are run by guardians, who are a great source of local information and advice. This resource is of real benefit to Alpine trail runners, as it allows a degree of self-sufficiency that is not dissimilar to that encountered in the UK mountains, despite the far greater altitudes.

A major factor to consider is the seasonal nature of Alpine trail running: during the winter months the snowline creeps all the way down into the valleys, limiting running at this time of year to all but the most experienced.

Trail kit

While every runner wants to move quickly and lightly in the mountains, it's essential that you carry enough kit to enable self-sufficiency – especially in case of changing weather and emergencies. Runners often query the obligatory equipment lists provided by race organisers, but it's important to note that these events are professionally organised, with medical assistance, shelters, aid stations and rescue plans in place. An autonomous runner should always carry the standard obligatory race kit as an absolute minimum, to cater for the fact that the race provisions and safety net are not in place.

Some of the easier and lower-altitude routes in this book can be undertaken wearing road shoes and your normal running clothing, as well as a small running pack, but as you venture higher into the mountains you'll need more clothing and trail-specific footwear.

The choice of shoes for trail running is open to endless debate, but what you should look for is a good traction grip (especially on rock), a rock plate in the sole, and increased protection around the toe box.

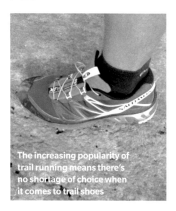

The increasing popularity of trail running means there's no shortage of choice when it comes to trail shoes

Features such as mud or off-trail performance don't matter so much in the Alps, as the trails are fairly established and well drained underfoot. Brands that dominate the European market are Salomon, La Sportiva and Inov8. Rugged mountain trails are no place for minimalist or barefoot shoes, although an increasing number of runners are using maximalist shoes such as Hoka's.

A decent running bag is essential, as there's a fair bit of kit to take each day that needs to be readily accessible while you're on the move. Key features that a runner might look for are a capacity of up to 12L, a bladder or water bottle pouch system, accessible stow pockets for snacks, a whistle for emergencies, and compartments to store waterproofs and other items. When purchasing a bag, try packing it with your running kit and then testing it for fit to ensure that it doesn't move on your back.

Poles are another useful, if not essential, piece of trail running kit. Make sure they are portable (some fold down or retract to fit easily into or onto your bag) and have a grip covering an extended section of the shaft to allow for different hand heights on traverses of steeper terrain. There's a wide range of running poles, from telescopic to z-poles and now rigid grip poles, to choose from. Good brands to consider are Leki, Grivel, Black Diamond and A2-16. 'Adapting to the Alps' outlines some of the benefits and techniques of running with poles in the Alps.

You're strongly advised to take an altimeter when running in the Alps, as they're a very useful navigational tool and allow you to focus more on the running than poring over a map and compass. Relatively cheap units are built into robust digital watches, such as the Suunto Vector, and there are also mobile phone apps to consider, such as View Ranger or Strava. GPS units provide altitude figures, but while they don't need recalibrating like watches, the signal might be too weak to give accurate information, such as when you're close to a cliff and satellite signals are hidden by the topography.

Equipment checklist

The following list includes all the items you could possibly run with in the Alps. Don't assume you have to carry it all: runs in different seasons, altitudes and weathers will have vastly contrasting requirements. Equip yourself according to your chosen route and the likely or possible conditions, but bear in mind that the safety kit should be carried as standard.

Basics
- Trail running shoes
- Socks
- Shorts or tights
- T-shirt/long-sleeved top
- Running gloves
- Buff/cap
- Beanie hat
- Sunglasses
- Suncream
- Water bottle/bladder
- Food

Optional items
- Running poles
- Compression calf guards
- Running gaiters

Insulation and waterproofs
- Waterproof gloves/mitts
- Thermal layer
- Windproof jacket
- Waterproof jacket and trousers

First aid
- Zinc-oxide/strapping tape
- Wound dressing
- Blister plasters (Compeed or similar)
- Anti-chafing gel

Safety
- Mountain rescue numbers (see Appendix A)
- Compass

- GPS
- Altimeter
- Map
- Guidebook
- Whistle
- Survival blanket
- Head torch
- Batteries
- Phone

Personal
- Passport
- Money
- Bank card
- Insurance
- Toilet roll
- Rubbish bag

Winter or altitude trails
- Instep crampons
- Ice axe
- Rope
- Sling
- Karabiners
- Blizzard bag

Adapting to the Alps

No matter how experienced you are as a trail runner, your first running trip in the Alps will be an amazing experience. However, there are a few things that runners used to smaller hills may find useful when preparing for and running in the Alpine mountains.

Getting the best from your body

Build up your core strength for Alpine trail running, as it is key to keeping you stable and improving your reaction speeds to trip hazards on the mountains. Learn to adapt your running style to use different muscle groups in turn so as to rest others. For example, using your gluteus muscles for ascents will rest your quadriceps for a descent.

When running uphill, try to adjust the amount you raise your feet with each step to avoid wasted energy. Your shoes should skim just above the surface of the rocks in order to reduce impact and over-lifting. Where there's a lot of height gain and your calf muscles are hurting, try running more flat-footed for a while; this moves the stress from the lower leg to the quadriceps and gluteus muscle groups. Once the lactic acid or cramp has left your lower leg, you can run on your forefoot again.

Look carefully at the profile of the route you plan to run. Try and project where you can recuperate, and where you might need to adjust your technique. Knowing what's coming next enables you to manage your energy output better when running uphill.

Be aware that on longer trail runs it may be more efficient and safer to walk on some steeper sections than it is to run. While you might never dream of doing this on a half marathon or a fell race, it's sensible and often necessary on Alpine peaks. Even the winners of races walk some sections.

Food and water

On longer runs it's important to listen to your body and to supply it with

On the trail to the Plan d'Aiguille (Route 1)

the food types it's craving. Don't rely on gels alone, as they'll make you nauseous. On trail races the food stations supply a wide range of food, including bananas, cakes, cheese, dried meats, energy bars, chocolate and fruits. On longer runs your body needs complex and simple carbohydrates, as well as fats. A mixture of all of these elements is required.

Running with 1L of water per 1000m of height gain is a reasonable equation. Access to water on your route will depend on its geology and aspect; you can't always rely on plentiful sources for topping up. On some routes you'll pass water troughs where you can refill your water bottle – look out for *eau potable* (French) or *acqua potabile* (Italian) signs to ensure that the water is drinkable. Be especially careful in selecting water sources in areas where animals are grazing

Many of the routes in this guide go past mountain refuges where it's possible to buy refreshments.

Running at higher altitudes

Don't be tempted to run straight up one of the highest routes in this guidebook without acclimatising properly first. Symptoms of altitude sickness include shortness of breath, headaches, nausea, loss of balance and loss of appetite; most trail runners experience these things fairly regularly on their training runs anyway, so acclimatisation is very tricky to differentiate.

The key suggestion is that you increase your maximum altitude in stages over your stay. Most people feel no effects at 2000m, but you could build up a maximum height by between 300–500m each day. If you ensure that you hydrate well, protect yourself from the sun and wear suitably protective sunglasses, you'll be stacking the odds in your favour that you don't misdiagnose any symptoms of altitude sickness. If you do suspect you're struggling with the altitude, running downhill is the quickest way to alleviate any issues.

To enjoy Alpine trail running you don't have to be superhumanly fit. You need to be in good condition for running, but also determined and highly adaptable. Adapt your output to the terrain, altitude and length of your run. Some of the best trail runners aren't the fittest or the fastest, but those with the most tricks up their sleeves, who save energy wherever possible. Remember that laziness and efficiency are the same thing re-marketed!

Tackling the terrain

When ascending steeper rock steps, or when ascending metal foot plates fixed to the rock, try not to climb on your tiptoes facing directly into the rock. There are three key reasons for this: firstly, you're putting a lot of strain on your calf muscles which will tire them for running; secondly, you get more traction by turning your foot *across* a foothold; and thirdly, by turning sideways you're more stable and able to look around for the next moves to make. When scrambling on steeper ground, always try to keep three points of contact at all times so that a slip doesn't become a fall. (Consider wearing gloves to protect your hands.)

On descent, it's easy to lose your pace by braking too much. Try to let the gradient do the work for you, keeping an eye on the descent rate of your altimeter if you have one. Dropping -25m/min is a fast but sustainable rate. Keep your focus for trip hazards while revelling in the pace of the descent. You may encounter forest trails, so beware slippery tree roots – especially if it's wet. If you see a trip hazard, push upwards and over it, rather than braking to avoid it. Use your momentum to keep yourself safe. If you feel you're falling, try not to brace for impact but let yourself roll; most fall injuries result from runners sticking their limbs out in an attempt to stop their fall.

Running poles
It's rare to see a fell runner with poles in the UK, yet on the start line of UTMB over 90% of all runners will be carrying poles. The scale and nature of the Alpine landscape – its steepness, often combined with rough terrain – makes poles particularly useful. You could be running up a slope that's got more vertical ascent than any peak in your home country.

On ascent the poles improve your posture and breathing, as well as aiding rhythm and efficiency. This

Many runners consider poles essential in the Alps (Route 37)

will in turn aid your recovery, meaning you're better rested to keep a good pace on the steeper sections. In descent, the poles will aid balance and take some stress off the leg muscles and joints – it's thought you can reduce the impact on your knees by around 30% using poles.

You can practise using poles in descent by planting them together to leap over rocks or obstacles, or by planting singly, well ahead of you, to pivot or brace around a corner. Beware never to use wrist straps without a good fall release system, as in the event of a tumble a radial fracture of the wrist is likely.

If you opt to run with poles, consider wearing Nordic walking or fingerless gloves to protect your hands from blistering between your thumb and fingers, which is typically the point that gets most abrasion.

Night running

Some of the routes in this book, and the main mountain marathon events, involve running through the night due to their length. Be aware that although LED lights are good, they give a 2D effect, so depth perception is reduced. The net effect is that most runners move slower in darkness, so invest in the best light that you can afford, and practise night running to improve your speed.

Mountain skills

To be a safe mountain runner you'll need exactly the same skills set as an autonomous hiker, in terms of ability on broken mountain terrain, navigation in poor visibility, selecting the best route for the forecast, and remaining adaptable to your performance and the actual mountain conditions. It's far outside the scope of this book to cover all those elements, but don't assume that trail running is simply running that happens to be in the mountains. Good mountain skills and judgement are required at all times.

The key point to remember is that you shouldn't ever be afraid to adapt

your plans. The enjoyment of trail running doesn't necessarily come from a particular objective such as a pass or summit, but from the running itself. If you aren't feeling up to the objective, or the conditions rapidly change, don't feel pressured to continue; adapt your plans accordingly.

Navigation

Fortunately the paths are well signposted and marked in the Alps, so it's hard to lose your way. This guidebook contains clear maps to help with your route planning, with numbered waypoints corresponding to the route descriptions, but it's important to carry a full map of the area at all times for extra detail, and to run with just that in your hand or tucked into an easily accessible pocket on the front of your running bag. Relevant sheet maps are listed in the information box at the start of each route, and the Maps section (above) provides details of where the maps can be bought. If you use an altimeter to help navigate, you should recalibrate it frequently (many path junctions have spot heights on the map), as a navigational error could have serious consequences.

In the unlikely event that you do get lost, return to the last known point and work out where you went wrong, as once you're lost, errors tend to compound themselves. If you're unsure of your navigation or mountain skills, consider being led by a qualified professional guide: in

Old signposts in the forest (Route 18)

PLATEAU D'ASSY

LAC VERT

Summit signpost on Mont de l'Arpille (Route 26)

France the legal qualification to look for is a UIMLA International Mountain Leader – and ideally someone who is also an experienced trail runner and a personal trainer.

Using this guide

At the start of each route description is an information box giving the key facts about the route, including the start and end point, distance covered, ascent and descent involved, level of difficulty, the length of time it's likely to take, the highest altitude reached, and details of relevant maps, public transport and the best time of year to attempt it.

Distance

In trail running, the total distance is not always the best measure of a route – although it's provided in this book as a means of helping you gauge your performance, or to select a suitable run. Distances are given in metric, to fit with maps and electronic devices from GPS units to watches, as well as in imperial. In fact the distance is less important to a mountain trail runner than the altitude gain or technical grade of the route.

Ascent/descent

The cumulative total ascent and descent is provided for each route. This is especially important for runners who may be stronger in one aspect or another. For example, those who try and avoid long descents due to niggling injuries in the knees might look for a split of more ascent

Descending snow from Le Brévent (Route 5)

Non-technical singletrack leaving Tre-le-Champ village (Route 8)

to descent. On several routes an opt-out point at a cable car is detailed, so you can elect whether to continue or descend. All altitudes are quoted in metres in order to tally with maps and altimeters.

Grades of trail

Also included is the grading of the run, which has been categorised into the following levels so that you can easily select a route that suits your aspirations for the day.

Trail running

These runs follow paths that are marked on the IGN maps, and often include sections of GR (*Grand Randonnée*) routes such as the GR5 or Tour du Mont Blanc. They vary from single track, where runners have to run in single file, to wider trails where you can run alongside others. There will be a good level of signage, so navigation is rarely an issue. These trails help link together the vast mountain hut and cable car network that surrounds Mont Blanc.

Fell running

While this style of running is more suited to the UK mountains and fells, it's where you often avoid trails and paths to take more direct lines across country, to speed your progress. Fell running is rarer in the Alps due to the density of the trees up to the treeline at around 1800m. Above that you soon encounter glacial moraines and very steep ground, and so trails

Level	Trail running	Fell running	Skyrunning
1	Well-marked wider trails, equivalent of UK bridle-ways, with little steeper ground	n/a	n/a
2	Well-established trails, with some small areas of rough ground, well signposted	Off-track between distinct identifiable points, non-technical ground underfoot	n/a
3	Single-track trails, with some steeper ground and rougher underfoot, well signposted	Steeper sections, and rougher underfoot, where care is needed to avoid slipping	Easier scrambling, or small sections of fixed equipment, or easy snow patches
4	Single-trail path, and less marked mountain terrain including scree and boulders	Venturing onto steeper ground, where hands might be used on steep pitches	Exposed with scrambling and mountain skills needed, or steeper snow patches
5	Very indistinct path over broken mountain terrain that is difficult to run over	Very steep or slippery slopes where route choice and navigation is essential	Very aerial route, with lots of exposure and significant amount of fixed equipment

follow the paths of least resistance. A few of the routes in this guidebook do involve sections of fell running where solid navigation is required.

Skyrunning

This type of trail is generally found on higher, steeper terrain, where there are few if any signposts and the ground underfoot is often rough. You'll encounter more exposure and drop-offs, where more advanced mountain skills and good footwork are essential. You'll often reach a mountain summit on this type of route, and some easy scrambling may be required. Some fixed equipment, such as metal handrails, ladders, chains, or fixed rope may also be used.

Timings

The average running time has been given for each route, as this will provide a meaningful gauge for most readers. The intention is that the times will suit the majority, but as you progress through the itineraries in this guidebook you'll quickly decide whether you need to adapt the timings to your own speed. A calculation that works well for shorter runs is 8km/h plus 1hr per 1000m ascended. For example, the Mont Blanc marathon is 42km, so 5hr 15min as the crow flies. There's 2500m vertical, so another 2hr 30min should be added. This gives a guesstimate of 7hr 45min,

with a comfortable margin before the 9hr cut-off for the official race in June.

Season

It's possible to run every day of the year in the Alps, but the key variable that dictates when it's best to tackle many routes is the snow cover, which can appear as early as late September, with patches sometimes lingering well into July even at relatively low altitudes. Running on snow is delightful, but is not without its hazards – especially the risks of sliding and avalanche. With this is mind, a suggested ideal season for each running route is provided, where typically the snow has disappeared completely or remaining patches have consolidated and stabilised and are passable by a competent trail runner.

Abbreviations and place names

Within the route descriptions 'left' and 'right' have been abbreviated to L and R, with LH and RH for 'left-hand' and 'right-hand', and 'straight ahead' to SA. Similarly, the four points of the compass have been abbreviated to N, S, E and W, and the well-known running and trekking trails and races are referred to by their acronyms (UTMB: Ultra Trail du Mont Blanc, TMB: Tour du Mont Blanc, TDS: Traces des Ducs de Savoie). Significant place names along the way are shown in **bold** to aid navigation.

Trail running above Planpraz (Routes 7 and 8)

FRANCE

Route 1
Mer de Glace

Start/Finish	Montenvers railway station, Chamonix (1035m/3395ft)
Distance	15.3km (9½ miles)
Ascent	1260m (4135ft)
Descent	1270m (4165ft)
Grade	Trail running, Level 2 (with descent from Plan d'Aiguille, Level 3)
Time	4hr 30min
High point	Le Signal (2204m/7230ft)
Maps	IGN 3630 Chamonix 1:25,000, Rando Editions A1 Pays du Mont Blanc 1:50,000
Public transport	Train/bus to Chamonix
Season	Mid June to October

This is perhaps the most classic trail run in Chamonix for ease of access and views. The scenery is wild and spectacular, although the runner does not encounter terrain where mountain skills are required. This level of accessibility makes it justifiably popular with both runners and hikers, but the variety of gradient and terrain makes it perfect for running. The upper section of the route follows a balcony trail perched well over a kilometre above the Chamonix valley, which is laid out like a map far below. If you only run one route in the region, make it this one.

Safety

This route should never be undertaken outside the suggested season – especially after heavy snow – as you cross several major avalanche gullies, such as below the Glacier de Nantillons.

---

1 From the Montenvers rack and pinion railway terminus in Chamonix, cross the main road towards Les Planards car park. To the R of a children's play park is a steep jeep track running up alongside the summer luge. Follow the signs for Les Mottets, and the trail crosses the Montenvers

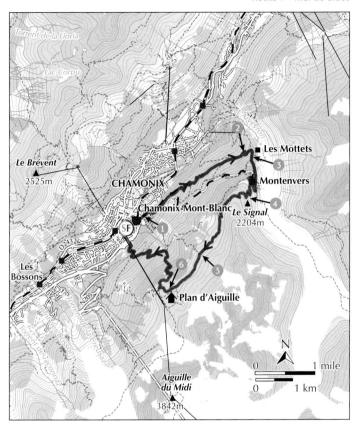

mountain railway track next to a farm before a few zig-zags give way to a long, steady, rising traverse.

2 At the end of the traverse the ground becomes rocky underfoot, and there are two switchbacks as you ascend a steeper step just below **Les Mottets**. Here you'll find a small wooden café kiosk and a view over the snout of the Mer de Glace glacier to the imposing Aiguille du Dru towering above. The trail turns sharply R here; follow painted dots up the glacially scoured rocks and lateral moraines to reach two short ladders that climb over two boulders.

Reaching Le Signal above the Mer de Glace

③ At a path junction soon after, take the L fork, signposted to Montenvers. The path winds among boulders for a short while, then the trail improves to give way to a series of stone steps that climb alongside the glacier. After about 10 minutes you'll pass beneath the lines of the cable car that takes tourists down from Montenvers top station to the ice cave tunnelled into the glacier. Spot the train station above you, and at the path junction turn R and follow the larger path up to **Montenvers**. There's a café here, as well as a tap on the end wall of the station where you can fill up your water bottles.

Pacing long ascents

Pacing on the ascent is the key to enjoying this run to its full potential, and many find an altimeter useful as a gauge for monitoring your ascent rate. Fast runners may well be able to maintain climbs at 20m/min, and at 10m/min you may be better off walking rather than running. A steady running pace gaining around 15m/min is sustainable, and allows you to avoid going anaerobic and into a stop-start sequence.

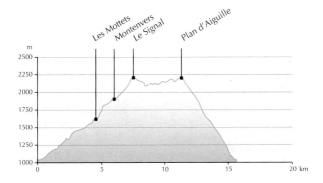

Pass the station and go under the tracks to reach the Victorian Montenvers hotel. Here you can truncate your run by following signs down to Chamonix via Le Caillet, but to continue on the main route, turn sharp L up towards Le Signal. The views down to the Mer de Glace, and ahead to the Grandes Jorasses, just get better and better as you ascend via a long traverse and then a series of switchbacks.

④ **Le Signal** is the high point of the run, and it's worth taking a minute to look at the cairns that have been erected here to honour those lost in the mountains, before following signs across to the Plan d'Aiguille. The terrain is rolling in this section, so you'll gain and lose height in roughly equal measure, but the route is very runnable and so the pace can quicken now that you've done the main height gain.

⑤ Run below the granite spires of the Aiguilles de Chamonix, noticing ahead the cable car station on the Plan d'Aiguille. (About halfway along to the Plan, look out for a small path off to the R, signed for Chamonix via the Alpages de Blatière: this could serve as an escape route for those wanting to truncate their run by an hour.)

Continue towards Plan d'Aiguille, crossing a series of streams and then following a signpost to the **Refuge du Plan d'Aiguille** mountain hut. Refreshments can be obtained at the hut, and the cakes are highly recommended! (A final escape route option is to ascend from the hut to the Plan d'Aiguille cable car station and take the téléphérique down to Chamonix.)

Mid-traverse on the Plan d'Aiguille

6 If you're happy to run the remainder of the route, turn sharp R just before the hut and descend the trail steeply towards Chamonix. Take care on the first 100m of descent as it involves steep, rocky ground that's exposed and often quite greasy when wet or frosty. After 10 minutes the trail becomes less steep and is easier to run, and at 1800m you reach the treeline and will find the path more cushioned underfoot.

Keep following the signs towards Chamonix and the Aiguille du Midi car park. This section can be run quickly, and you soon emerge from the woods behind the Midi cable car. Turn R along Rue Lyret in front of the cable car station, and at the first roundabout turn R again. Run 200m along the road, then turn L just after a car park and continue on the footpath along the train lines to arrive back at the Montenvers train station in **Chamonix**.

Route 2
River track to Argentière

Start	Main square, Chamonix (1035m/3395ft)
Finish	Railway station, Argentière (1246m/4087ft)
Distance	8.8km (5½ miles)
Ascent	221m (725ft)
Descent	10m (35ft)
Grade	Trail running, Level 1
Time	1hr 20min
High point	Argentière (1246m/4088ft)
Maps	IGN 3630 Chamonix 1:25,000, Rando Editions A1 Pays du Mont Blanc 1:50,000
Public transport	Train/bus to Chamonix and from Argentière
Season	March to December

If you're looking for a shorter run, without any significant gradients or altitude gain but in beautiful scenery and with plenty of opt-out points, this is the trail for you. It's ideal on bad weather days, when you need to keep out of the mountains. Perhaps its greatest advantage is that due to the low altitude, this trail has the longest runnable season of any route in this guidebook.

1 Start in Chamonix town square, next to the statue of Balmat and Saussure, and follow the river upstream keeping the water to your L. As you leave the town centre you pass the school and sports centre. Cross the river by the footbridge just after the tennis courts, then cross a second bridge that brings you out next to a smaller tributary separating your trail from the road

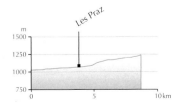

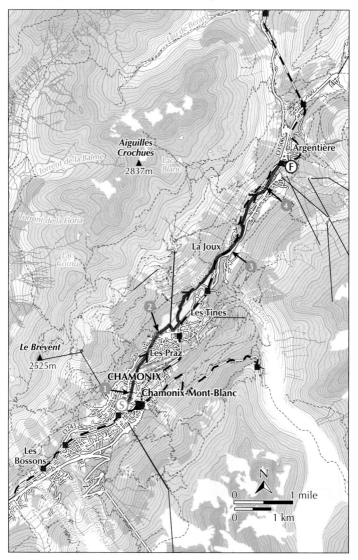

Safety

This route is objectively very safe and can be undertaken in all weathers – except when the river is in flood. At such times the banks are liable to flooding, and several footbridges over tributaries may be dangerous.

Nearing the village of Les Tines

Gear for easier routes

Poles aren't necessary on this route, as the trails are wide, and you don't need them to safeguard any traverse or for a steep ascent. The route is very runnable and can even be undertaken using road shoes. It's a good idea to alternate between different pairs of shoes each day to allow the cushioning to recover and to dry out fully.

to Les Praz. Run along this wide trail towards Les Praz, crossing several roads that turn off across the river.

2 On reaching **Les Praz**, turn L across the road bridge and then immediately R, and follow the trail to the Flégère cable car. Cross into the car park, and at the far end turn L along the road to Argentière until you reach the entrance to a golf club on your L. Turn in here, and at the end of the car park take a track that leads past the driving range and then towards Paradis des Praz.

The trail here leads onwards to pass the hamlet of **Les Tines** before ascending above the river, which is now down to your R. At every path junction, opt for the lower track on the R, and you're soon sandwiched between the train track to your L and the river to your R.

3 Cross the road to **La Joux**, and then the trail makes its way up the valley towards Argentière. The woods open up and you get more of a view ahead to Le Tour and across to Le Lavancher.

4 At **Argentière** you hit the main road on a corner; turn L and follow it uphill to pass beneath the trail tracks. Here, on the L is the bus stop for a return to Chamonix, or the railway station is in the building on the R.

Route 3
Merlet

Start	SNCF station, Chamonix (1035m/3395ft)
Finish	SNCF station, Servoz (815m/2673ft)
Distance	15.5km (9¾ miles)
Ascent	710m (2330ft)
Descent	930m (3050ft)
Grade	Trail running, Level 3
Time	2hr 45min
High point	Merlet (1520m/4986ft)
Maps	IGN 3531 St Gervais 1:25,000, Rando Editions A1 Pays du Mont Blanc 1:50,000
Public transport	Bus/train to Chamonix, train from Servoz
Season	April to November

Despite its proximity to Chamonix and Les Houches – the two largest towns in the Chamonix valley – this trail is a delightful exploration of the forest balcony paths all the way to Servoz. You'll pass through traditional Savoyard farming villages, such as Montvauthier, and a series of *alpages* (pastures) near Le Coupeau. This run will appeal to lovers of nature; it's a particular delight in late summer as the leaves are starting to turn.

1 With the Chamonix SNCF station behind you, run straight down the road ahead and across the river to the wooden clock tower. Turn L here onto the main pedestrian high street through Chamonix and follow it through the square and past all the shops to a roundabout. Cross this and go SA on the road to **Les Gaillands** – a popular rock climbing crag on the R, set back less than 100m from the road.

2 Veer towards the crag on the path, which skirts between lakes and plunges into the woods. Run past a forest high ropes circuit, then a cluster of houses and a small car park on the L, and turn sharply R up the hillside, signposted for Parc Merlet. At a path junction at 1105m, turn L to reach the Petit Balcon trail that zig-zags and makes a long, rising traverse across the hillside.

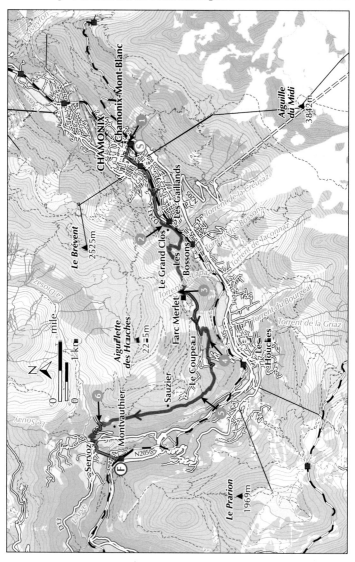

Safety

This route has a long season and can be run whenever it's snow-free. The key safety concern is crossing the couloir just before Merlet, where avalanches from above can be a risk, so it's a case of judging the conditions above the route. If you're unsure, you can follow the river track all the way from Les Gaillands to Les Houches SNCF station, then turn right and follow the signposts up to the statue of Christ Roi and meet the route there. This completely avoids the Merlet gully and is objectively safer, albeit with far less elevation.

3 Cross a series of small streams that cut down the mountainside, but don't count on any of these as a water source as many are ephemeral. As you approach the large gully of the **Torrent de Lapaz** the trail is quite exposed, so run carefully. On the far side of the stream the trail climbs to reach **Parc Merlet**. Turn L and run down the road, continuing past the viewpoint until you see a sign off to the L for the TMB track and Christ Roi. Follow the trail to the concrete statue, which looks like a very small 1960s Soviet-style version of Rio de Janeiro's Christ the Redeemer statue!

4 After a quick look around, take the trail towards the village of **Le Coupeau**, and when you reach the road follow it directly, or via a series of paths between the corners, until you reach the hamlet of **Le Grand Clos** at 2000m. Take the path heading W off the apex of the road corner, and at the trail junction take the R turn upwards towards Morand.

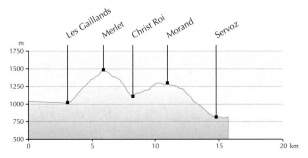

Traversing the trails above Le Coupeau

Dealing with dogs

When running in the Alps, you're likely to encounter large white Pyrenean Mountain Dogs guarding flocks of sheep or goats. They're often called *pastous* or *patous* – a derivative of the old French word *pastre*, for shepherd. They're becoming increasingly rare due to the diminished risk of flocks being attacked by bears, wolves or lynx in the region, and they shouldn't cause a runner any concern. If a dog thinks you're a potential threat it will position itself between you and the flock to assess you. Stop running and walk slowly past, averting your eyes. Remain calm and quiet, and don't make any sudden movements or wave your running poles. The dog should return to the flock, and you can continue slowly by before starting to run again when you're at least 100m away.

5 Just above these chalets you reach another junction; run SA towards **Sauzier**. This is a great section of the run, as you follow an increasingly exposed and narrow forest trail. There's little chance of slipping, but there are cliffs above and below you in places, so keep focused and watch your footwork.

6 Eventually the trail starts to descend and you reach the village of **Montvauthier**, often passing *patous* guarding flocks of sheep. Run down the road, with the path cutting corners, to reach **Servoz** next to the entrance of the Gorges de Diosaz. Follow signs for the village centre, then turn L at the mini-roundabout and run down the long straight to the Servoz SNCF train station.

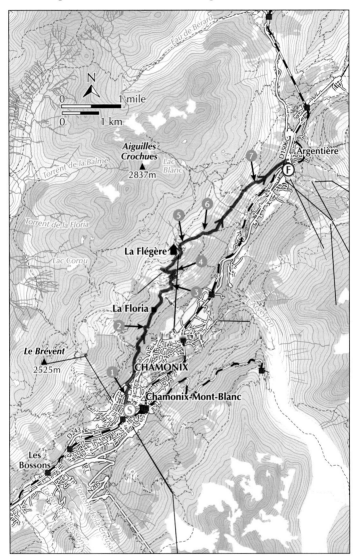

Route 4
La Flégère

Start	Savoy ski slopes, Chamonix (1035m/3395ft)
Finish	SNCF station, Argentière (1246m/4087ft)
Distance	10.8km (6¾ miles)
Ascent	810m (2675ft)
Descent	610m (2000ft)
Grade	Trail running, Level 2
Time	2hr 15min
High point	La Flégère (1877m)
Maps	IGN 3630 Chamonix 1:25,000, Rando Editions A1 Pays du Mont Blanc 1:50,000
Public transport	Train/bus from Argentière
Season	May to October

These trails are very well marked and frequented, so if your navigation skills aren't great it's a good choice, and it's also a perfect run when the weather's poor above the treeline, as you're above it for less than half an hour in total. What marks this run out are the great views across the valley to the Aiguilles de Chamonix and the glaciers. There's also a nice mix of wide trails and some well-established single track.

Safety

Don't be tempted to run this route out of season: part of the run is in a ski area that's out of bounds to pedestrians (and runners) when open for skiers, and some of the bridges on the route are removed out of season to stop them being swept away in winter floods or avalanches.

1. The Savoy nursery slopes are situated just behind the church in Chamonix; run across the field to the R of the Balcons du Savoy apartment buildings and there's a mini-roundabout on the road just behind them. Turn R here towards Le Nants and run along the road for a few hundred metres until a small road winds off to the L. On its first corner, take a wide track ahead that

leads up towards the Petit Balcon Sud.

(2) Keep an eye out for a path junction, where you bear L up towards La Floria. A jeep track leads all the way up to the chalet **La Floria** where you can make an early pit stop for refreshments and enjoy the panoramic views across to Les Drus and down the Chamonix valley. From La Floria, keep running upwards, ignoring the path down to Les Praz, and contour around a large gully.

Chalet La Floria in full bloom

(3) After passing two streams you arrive at a path junction; turn uphill and climb a series of switchbacks until you reach a jeep track. Cross this and ahead is the trail on the far side, which ascends into the woods.

(4) The zig-zags twice bring you underneath the cables and pylon of the Flégère cable car. Keep ascending until you reach a ski piste (which is a jeep track in summer). Turn sharp R, and the path leads you gently upwards to reach **La Flégère**. Here you pass beneath the old mountain hut situated just

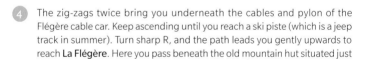

Gels or food?

Some runners depend on energy gels as their main source of fuel on the trail. If you have a dependence on gels, you need to be very consistent in terms of the regularity with which you take them, and you also need to drink enough water to help break down their sugars to release all the available energy. This balance is very hard to achieve, and so most runners find it easier to carry a mixture of slower-release energy foods such as cereal bars and flapjack, as well as gels for quick boosts on small sections.

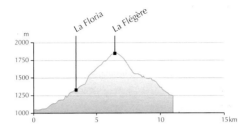

below the cable car building, so there's the opportunity for refreshments as well as the escape route option of the cable car if you're tired. Note that the cable car is normally the first in the valley to close in the event of high winds or storms, so don't rely on it.

5 Just beyond and below the hut is a reservoir – the water source for snow cannons in winter. Skirt around the lake to the L, and ahead of you is a long ski piste descending gently to the R. Run down this, keeping the chairlift cables to your R, and at the bottom end of the ski piste spot a trail heading off on the L. Take this, running onwards and down into the forest.

6 Ignore a turnoff to the R and continue down seemingly endless zig-zags until the trail suddenly flattens out at 1579m. Here turn L and enter a wonderful rolling traverse section of the run, crossing a metal bridge over the stream descending from Lac Blanc.

7 Ignore a turnoff to the L and follow the signs for Argentière, which you can see below in the valley floor. The path becomes a little rocky for a while, so watch your footing. As you arrive in **Argentière**, round a building to reach the main road. Turn R, and you'll soon see the SNCF train station on your L, with the bus stop directly opposite on your R.

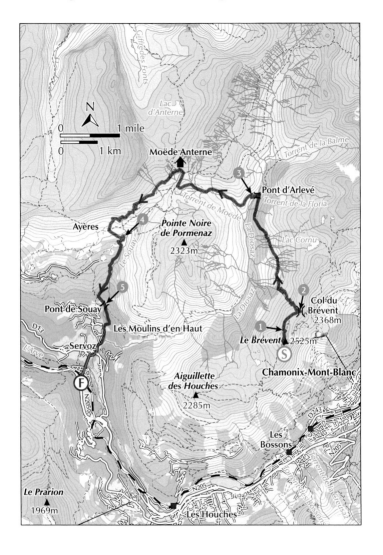

Route 5
Refuge Moëde Anterne

Start	Brévent cable car station (2525m/8284ft)
Finish	SNCF station, Servoz (815m/2673ft)
Distance	17.5km (11 miles)
Ascent	430m (1410ft)
Descent	2100m (6890ft)
Grade	Trail running, Level 3
Time	3hr 45min
High point	Brévent (2525m/8284ft)
Maps	IGN 3530 Samoëns 1:25,000, IGN 3530 ET Samoëns 1:25,000, Rando Editions A1 Pays du Mont Blanc 1:50,000
Public transport	Bus/train to Chamonix
Season	Mid July to September

If the hustle and bustle of Chamonix gets to you, and you want a quick escape into the wilderness well away from the crowds, this is the route to take. Within seconds of the start point the Chamonix valley is left from view and you're immersed in the unspoiled and undeveloped scenery of a nature reserve. It's rare to see more than a handful of people on this run, so it's a great choice if you want revel in solitude.

Safety

Don't undertake this run too early in the season, as the traverse from Brévent to the Col du Brévent is on north-facing slopes, which can hold steep icy snow patches into July. These are not safe to cross in trail running shoes without crampons or an ice axe, so get advice before you set out.

1 Exit the cable car station and follow the wide rubble track down a few corners until you reach rocky narrows, where you'll see a signpost to the Col du Brévent on the L. Here the path drops steeply over rocks on a single track; descend two small ladders over a rock step to gain a traverse across to the

R. Follow the dots of paint on the rocks, and after a small re-ascent reach the **Col du Brévent**.

(2) After admiring the view of Mont Blanc, framed by the pass, turn L and run through the rocky valley on a stone path. The track dips steeply on the L and you descend a series of zig-zags as the route becomes less exposed and more vegetated. There then follows a brilliant long, winding descent towards the **Pont Arleve**, passing through the ruins of a long-abandoned farm. Just before the bridge the trail becomes narrow and quite exposed to your L, so take extra care.

(3) On the far side of the bridge the path gains 200m quite quickly before the gradient relaxes to a steady incline up towards the **Moëde Anterne** mountain hut. In places it's quite wet underfoot, especially after rain. You can stop at the hut for refreshments and to refill your water bottle in the trough outside, and then follow the jeep track up behind the old hut building. This soon turns L to traverse the hillside; follow signposts towards **Ayères** and you'll pass the Pierre de L'Ours (Bear Rock) with a shepherd's hut built against it.

Below the Refuge Moëde Anterne

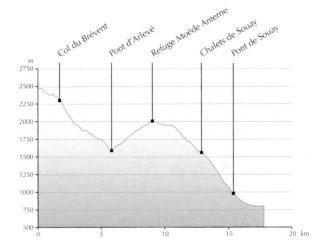

④ Keep an eye out for the sign to the Chalets de Souay (1569m), and descend past them. Soon after, on a hairpin in the track, take a turnoff to the L towards Barme Trappier and Servoz on single tracks through the forest. This is a delightful section, with small glades, dense woods and several small stream crossings. Ignore signs to Lac Vert and keep following signs for Servoz.

⑤ Reach the **Pont de Souay** at 981m; cross the bridge and ascend the track for a few hundred metres until a sign takes you off to the R on a single track leading to the traditional hamlet of **Les Moulins d'en Haut**, with its water-mills and wooden farm buildings. Join the road leading down to **Servoz** village, and at the crossroads go SA into the village centre. Turn L at the mini-roundabout to follow the long straight to finish at the train station.

Surviving 2000m descents

This run has a lot of descent in it, so to save your leg muscles (such as the quadriceps), let your weight shift to the forefoot rather than heel striking or mid-foot, and you'll reduce the braking effect and consequent impact on your legs with each stride.

🏃 59

Route 6
La Jonction

Start/Finish	SNCF station, Les Bossons (1012m/3320ft)
Distance	12.5km (7¾ miles)
Ascent/Descent	1530m (5020ft)
Grade	Trail running, Level 4 (with Skyrunning, Level 3, above 2000m)
Time	3hr 45min
High point	La Jonction (2589m/8494ft)
Maps	IGN 3531 St Gervais 1:25,000, Rando Editions A1 Pays du Mont Blanc 1:50,000
Public transport	Train/bus to Les Bossons
Season	July to September

This route takes you into the mountains, and they seem close enough to touch from the top at La Jonction, where the glaciers of Bossons and Taconnaz split apart. Steep gradients and big exposure are encountered in this harsh yet stunning scenery. The route shares the first part of a trail that Jacques Balmat and Michel-Gabriel Paccard took when they made the first ascent of Mont Blanc in 1786, making it one of historical importance for Alpinists.

Safety

Do not contemplate this route if there's any snow at all remaining. It's easy to view the upper section and the east-facing gullies from Chamonix, and you can get a perfect view onto the whole route from the cable car station at the summit of Le Brévent. The higher part of the trail is a notorious accident hotspot with hikers attempting to ascend the route out of season. Also beware of undertaking this route if it's raining, as the upper rocks become very slippery, especially in running shoes.

---

1 Exit the train station at Les Bossons, and at the main road turn R then almost immediately L up a side road that leads past the Aiguille du Midi hotel and on top of the highway underpass. On the far side, follow the road on the R

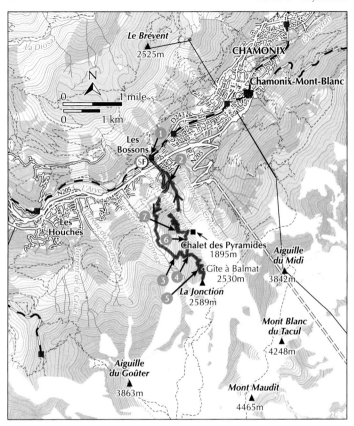

and soon reach the bridge over the **Torrent des Bossons**. Cross the bridge and stay on the road running steeply uphill.

2 At the first corner the chair lift lines are ahead of you. After two switchbacks, pass the top of the Olympic ski jump in the hamlet of Le Mont and follow the road to a wide L bend at 1190m, where a track cuts off R up the hillside and works its way deep into the valley below the Taconnaz glacier, ascending the lateral moraines on the L side of the valley as you look upwards.

Aiguille du Midi from La Jonction

La Jonction
alt.2589 m

3 Just above 1700m the trail veers L to ascend the hillside via short zig-zags towards a pass below Mont Corbeau. A few turns below the col, a track joins in from the L: this will be your descent track later, so if carrying a GPS unit it's well worth waymarking this point. (Don't worry if you aren't, as it's sign-posted, but remember to keep an eye out for it.)

4 As you reach the col, cross onto the far side of the mountain. There follows a nice rising traverse across the grassy hillside, which is a treat to run. Landscapes don't come much more stunning than this, and the vast bulk of the Bossons glacier ahead is unforgettable. At the end of the traverse the path turns sharp R, and there are some sections of fixed equipment up a rock step.

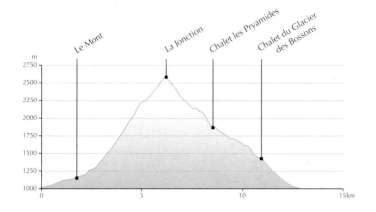

⑤ Regain the ridgeline above Mont Corbeau to embark on the steepest section of this trail. The route follows a series of painted markings on the rock, up a series of rock steps. It's never difficult to find your way, but if you've ever gone more than 20m without seeing a paint blob you need to retrace your steps.

The rock gives way to a boulder field and the gradient eases off slightly as you approach the massive boulders of Gîte à Balmat at 2530m, where the first ascensionists of Mont Blanc bivouacked for the night on their climb. A plaque affixed to one of the boulders marks this historic occasion.

After passing between the rocks, head up R to reach the summit of **La Jonction** at 2589m. Here the view up to the Aiguille du Midi is vertiginous and stupendous, as are the colours of the icefall descending from Mont Blanc. Don't

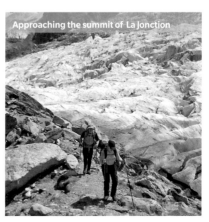

Approaching the summit of **La Jonction**

63

> ## Running near glaciers
>
> When running close to glaciers you need to plan for the micro-climate that they generate. Katabatic winds are the cool downdraughts caused by an air mass being chilled and sinking down glacial basins; it's worth taking an extra windproof layer when running next to or below glaciers to counter their effects.

be tempted to scramble onto the glacier surface, as it's complex and crevassed. If anyone falls into a crevasse without wearing a harness, rescue extraction is virtually impossible.

(6) After taking in the view, and taking photos, retrace your route all the way back over the pass to the N of Mont Corbeau. Descend to the signpost that was noted earlier and turn R towards **Chalet des Pyramides** at 1895m, where there's a small buvette selling refreshments. (It's decorated with remnants of the Air India flight 245, the Malabar Princess, which crashed into the mountain in 1950.)

(7) Below the buvette there's an exposed traverse across a steep gully with fixed ropes in place. The trail descends steeply into the woods, and the switchbacks lead eventually to the Chalet du Glacier des Bossons at the top of the chairlift. Directly below this the path follows the L lateral moraine of the glacier, all the way down to the road near the road bridge. Here regain your route from earlier to return to **Les Bossons** train station.

Route 7
Chamonix Vertical KM

Start	Main square, Chamonix (1035m/3395ft)
Finish	Planpraz paraglider take-off area (2035m/6676ft)
Distance	3.8km (2½ miles)
Ascent	1000m (3280ft)
Descent	0m
Grade	Skyrunning, Level 4 (with 200m of Level 5)
Time	1hr
High point	Planpraz paraglider take-off area (2035m/6676ft)
Maps	IGN 3630 Chamonix 1:25,000, Rando Editions A1 Pays du Mont Blanc 1:50,000
Public transport	Train/bus to Chamonix
Season	May to October
Note	If you're running this route for a good time you probably won't carry much water, but note that there's no drinkable water at Planpraz cable car station, so take some money to buy refreshments at the café or consider taking a waist belt with a small water pouch.

Many of the routes in this guidebook have elevation gains of over 1000m, but this is the only one of exactly a vertical kilometre, and you can gauge yourself against the times recorded for this route in the Skyrunning World Championships. Each year the record has been broken; at the time of writing it was just over half an hour.

Safety

This route is south facing, so it dries out very quickly in the spring. From the centre of Chamonix you can view the whole route: don't attempt it if there's any snow on it at all, as remaining snow patches will be steep and slippery. If you're in any doubt you could recce the route by taking the cable car up to Planpraz, or ask the staff in the cable car station whether any other runners have been out on the race route already.

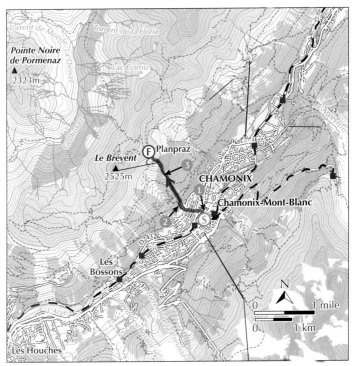

1. From next to the post office in Chamonix town square, run past the town hall and up the steep road directly behind the church. This takes you past the Mountain Rescue and Gendarmerie buildings and up to the base station of the Brévent cable car. Take the track to the L of the cable car buildings, where you'll see walk timings on a signpost. Follow the track until it curves around to the R beneath the cable car lines.

2. Look for a sharp turnoff on the L, and normally you'll see KMV (Kilometre Vertical) signs and arrows painted on the path. The zig-zags ascend the hillside directly beneath the cable car, whose bubbles will be moving above your head. At several points larger paths cross the route; ignore these and keep ascending.

Running on exposed terrain

Don't be tempted to take poles for this route, as the upper section is exposed and aerial, with fixed equipment. Keeping your hands free is essential so you can grip the cables for security. Via ferrata-style fingerless gloves are a good idea to protect your hands on the cables.

3   In the top third of the route, the path heads initially off to the R before doubling back on itself to gain the ridge crest. Move onto the LH side of the ridge, where you encounter the first sections of cable handrails. Ahead is a steep step with more fixed equipment, the sense of exposure increasing with every pace.

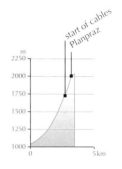

After ascending a steeper pitch, the cable car station of Planpraz comes into sight ahead, and you emerge through the cable car buildings to reach a large track. Cut around the buildings, and behind them the track curves up L. Run up this track to the finish, level with the **Planpraz** paraglider take-off zone, which is marked with a windsock and noticeboard. You've run your vertical kilometre; return to Chamonix by walking back to the cable car station and getting a lift down.

On the final section of cables of the Vertical KM

Route 8
Marathon du Mont Blanc

Start	Town hall, Chamonix (1035m/3395ft)
Finish	Planpraz paraglider take-off area (2050m/6725ft)
Distance	42km (27 miles)
Ascent	2722m (8930ft)
Descent	1674m (5490ft)
Grade	Trail running, Level 2 (2km of Level 3 over Posettes)
Time	7hr 15min
High point	Aiguillette des Posettes (2201m/7221ft)
Maps	IGN 3630 Chamonix 1:25,000, Rando Editions A1 Pays du Mont Blanc 1:50,000
Public transport	Bus/train to Chamonix, cable car from Planpraz
Season	Mid June to October
Note	During an actual race this route will be well equipped with drink and food stations, so you can carry very little. When running the route as a recce, ensure that you carry sufficient supplies, or some money to use at various shops or cafés.

This run closely follows the route of the Mont Blanc Marathon, so you can use it to train for the race, or you can undertake it to see how your time compares with the winners. The route explores some of the most classic trails of the Chamonix valley, and the highlight is running over the summit of the Aiguillette des Posettes, which provides a stunning viewpoint towards Mont Blanc. The finish is at Planpraz, perched over a kilometre above Chamonix.

For those wishing to split this route, it is described below in two stages – the best place to stop for the night being Vallorcine. This gives you two options, as you're next to the train station: either return by rail to your accommodation in Chamonix, or stay the night in the village. Gîte Mermoud is very traditional and centrally placed (www.cvmmontblanc.fr or tel +33 (0)450 546 003).

Stage 1 – Chamonix to Vallorcine
18.5km (11½ miles), 590m (1935ft) ascent, 365m (1195ft) descent, 2hrs

1 From in front of the town hall in Chamonix, turn L up the high street and go over the crossroad before turning R down to the sports centre. Pick up the Nordic ski trails, and soon leave the town behind as you thread through the woods towards **Les Bois**.

2 Pass the PGHM mountain rescue base, then ascend steeply towards the hamlet of **Le Lavancher** – a traditional village that's a delight to run through. Keep an eye out for a road on the R, signposted for Argentière.

Lavancher alpage and Mont Blanc

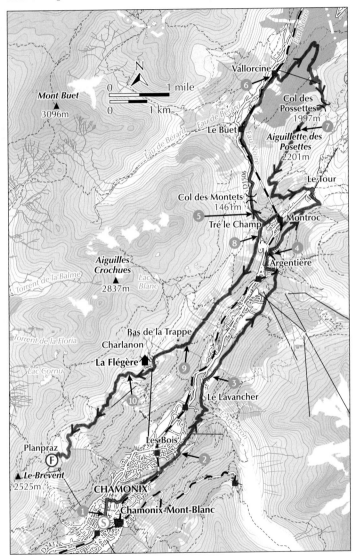

3 Cross the Lavancher *alpage* (pasture) before running a delightful rolling section of single track that emerges near the Grands Montets cable car. The trail leads through the tunnel under the home ski run and follows cross-country ski trails before turning L under the train line, reaching the oldest part of **Argentière**. (On race day there's a drink station here.)

4 Turn R before the church, and at the end of the jeep track turn R up to Le Planet. This short, steep ascent is over soon, and you traverse the fields to reach the Balcon Nord, which leads down to **Montroc**. Follow signs towards the Montroc train station, then take a little path that cuts up L over the top of the rail tunnel entrance. This leads to the picturesque hamlet of **Tré le Champ**, where you turn R to reach the road.

5 There's a trail just to the R of the road, leading through the nature reserve and over the **Col des Montets** (1461m). Soon after, there's a larger trail on the R called the Chemin des Diligences, which you follow all the way to **Le Buet** and onwards to **Vallorcine**. On race day there's a major drink and food station here, so runners can refuel before the big climb.

Stage 2 – Vallorcine to Planpraz
23.5km (14½ miles), 2130m (7000ft) ascent, 1310m (4300ft) descent, 5hr 15min

6 Just after the buildings in Vallorcine, turn sharp R up the field to the chalets, where the trail turns L into the forest. Keep on this steep forest track, following signs for the Col des Posettes. As you near the treeline the path joins a

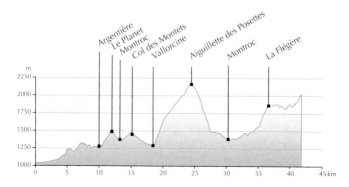

Crossing the Aiguillette des Posettes

large jeep track; turn R and follow it all the way up to the pass. You'll pass the top of the Vallorcine ski lift, and on race day there's a refreshment post on the **Col des Posettes**. From here the trail heads R to the obvious summit ahead, with the climb to the **Aiguillette des Posettes** providing a stunning panorama of the Mont Blanc massif.

7   Pass over the summit at 2201m and start the long descent of the ridge in the direction of Tré le Champ. There are a few steep sections and steps to negotiate, but the views provide ample reward. Descend below the treeline, keeping an eye out for a trail on the L to **Le Tour**. When you reach the village, run past the cable car and down the road a little before turning L towards the Le Tour glacier. Pass the Club Alpin Français (CAF) chalet, then as the road ends, turn R down the trail signposted to Montroc.

8   There's a short overlap with the trail you ran earlier as you return to **Tré le Champ**, where on race day there's a good food and drink station. Once you've eaten and rehydrated, pass through the village, following signs for the Aiguilles Rouges and La Flégère. Carefully cross the road and run up the

> ### Pace in the race
>
> This race is busy, and there are several bottleneck points, so it's important to set off quite quick to ensure that when your pace has settled you're ahead of the main pack and can keep a decent pace through the narrow sections.

path on the far side; it soon eases gradient and there's a wonderful section of single track leading to a path junction at 1579m.

9 Turn R and climb a long series of zig-zags, which brings you to **Bas de la Trappe**, the end of a ski run. Head directly up the ski run until you see the **La Flégère** cable car and hut ahead. Aim just to the L of the lowest buildings, where on race day there's the final refreshment post.

10 Beyond the hut, follow the signs towards Planpraz. This part of the trail is in the midst of the Aiguilles Rouges nature reserve. Descend a narrow, steep section shortly after Flégère, then there's a wonderful section of trail through the Charlanon gully, followed by a narrow rocky section before you reach a jeep track, which gets steeper and steeper on the final climb towards **Planpraz**.

The finish line is at the paraglider take-off zone at 2050m, and after all your efforts you're rewarded with one of the best views of the Bossons icefall and the summit of Mont Blanc.

Route 9
80km du Mont Blanc

Start/Finish	Town hall, Chamonix (1035m/3395ft)
Distance	83.7km (52 miles)
Ascent/Descent	6048m (19,840ft)
Grade	Trail running, Level 4 (and Skyrunning, Level 3)
Time	18hrs
High point	Col de la Terrasse (2631m/8631ft)
Maps	IGN 3630 Chamonix 1:25,000, IGN 3530 Samoëns 1:25,000, Rando Editions A1 Pays du Mont Blanc 1:50,000
Public transport	Train/bus to Chamonix
Season	Mid July to early September
Note	On this route you cross the border into Switzerland and back into France, so remember to carry your passport.

This route is raced once a year as part of the Marathon du Mont Blanc series, and was first run in 2013. It explores some remote areas such as the Tré les Eaux valley and Col de la Terrasse, as well as many popular balcony trails. For a running race, it tackles some quite technical terrain, where mountain skills and awareness are required.

The race is run in late June, when significant snow patches can often remain, so the organisers have three separate route plans that they select from to minimise risks to runners. The route description given here is that of the first edition of the race, which was run in June 2013. Note, however, that running this route before mid July is not recommended; it is best to wait until snow patches have melted completely or softened sufficiently.

The race route is described in two stages, with Vallorcine providing a stopover for those who would prefer not to undertake the whole circuit in one day. From there you can return by train to your accommodation in Chamonix, or stay in the village. Gite Mermoud is very traditional, and centrally placed (www.cvmmontblanc.fr or tel +33 (0)450 546 003).

Stage 1 – Chamonix to Vallorcine
44.5km (27¾ miles), 3860m (12,665ft) ascent, 3560m (11,680ft) descent, 9hr 30min

1 From Chamonix town hall, run past the church and up the hill on the road to the Brévent cable car station. Take the track to the L of the pylons, and just before the track heads R, turn sharp L and follow the signposts towards Bellachat. Be careful not to miss the R turn at 1382m, where you leave the wide track and ascend steep single tracks, soon leaving the treeline below. After a rocky ramp, spot the **Bellachat hut** above you at 2276m.

Bellachat refuge in the Aiguilles Rouges

75

(2) Directly behind the hut, the trail is signposted 'Brévent 2525m'; follow the ridge above the Lac du Brévent, with the pyramid shape of the Aiguille Verte ahead. Pass just below the **Brévent** cable car station over rocky ground and pick up the ski piste to accelerate down to **Planpraz**, where on race day the first refreshment station is located.

(3) Turning slightly L, follow the trails across to La Flégère. This is a section of the Tour du Mont Blanc, so it's well marked. Once past the hut at **La Flégère**

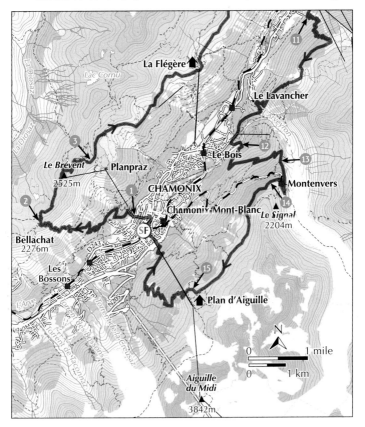

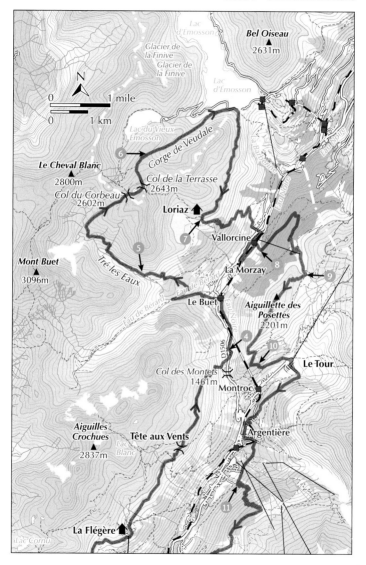

Running down snowfields from Le Brévent

you'll see the La Chavanne buvette to your L, where the trail leads onwards past the Chéserys chalet. Ascend over increasingly rocky trails to the **Tête aux Vents** before descending steeply to the **Col des Montets**.

4 Descend via easy trails to the R of the road to reach the hamlet of **Le Buet**, where you turn L and pass the ski lift of La Poya, and then the Cascade de Bérard, to enter the lower Bérard valley. Cross a bridge and double back on yourself to reach Sur le Rocher, then turn L and run to Les Granges, where you'll see a signpost to the L into the **Tré les Eaux** valley. This is the start of the most remote section of the route, and you're unlikely to see anyone for hours.

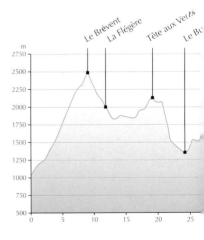

Kit for a big route

On this run you'll encounter high altitudes on several occasions, and if you're running for nearly a full day you'll need to carry enough clothing to allow for significant changes in temperature and weather. Take waterproof trousers as well as a good waterproof jacket with a hood. Even if you don't usually run with poles, they're highly recommended on this route for the rough terrain and snow patches as well as the significant height gains.

5 Follow a steep rocky section equipped with chains, then veer R to ascend more steeply to the **Col du Corbeau** at 2602m. Just beyond is a beautiful glacial lake, and beyond this you reach the **Col de la Terrasse** at 2643m before heading down L over the screes to reach the head of **Gorge de Veudale**. It feels as if you're running through a geology textbook in this section, with exposed strata and constantly changing rock types.

6 Descend the gorge, initially on the R bank and then, lower down, on the L bank. Ahead you can see **Lac d'Emosson** and its dam. Just before reaching the dam, turn R, signposted to Loriaz. The trail ascends via short sections of chains and metal steps before opening out to a wonderful trail leading to the **Loriaz hut**.

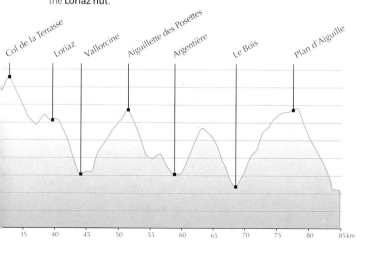

Traversing from Emosson to Loriaz

7 Below the hut is a cross on a huge boulder; the track turns off L just before it, plunging into the woods and down steeply towards Vallorcine. You emerge near the cable car station and make a loop up the river to cross at **La Morzay** before picking up the marathon track (Route 8), which you then follow back into **Vallorcine**.

Stage 2 – Vallorcine to Chamonix
39.2km (24½ miles), 2190m (7180ft) ascent, 2490m (8165ft) descent, 8hr 30min

8 Continuing on the marathon track, just after the buildings in Vallorcine turn sharp R up the field to the chalets, where the trail turns L into the forest. Keep on this steep forest track, following signs for the Col des Posettes. As you near the treeline the path joins a large jeep track; turn R and follow it all the way up to the pass, passing the top of the Vallorcine ski lift.

9 From here the trail heads R to the obvious summit ahead, with the climb to the **Aiguillette des Posettes** providing a stunning panorama of the Mont Blanc massif. Pass over the summit at 2201m and start the long descent of the ridge in the direction of Tré le Champ. There are a few steep sections and steps to negotiate, but the views provide ample reward.

(10) Descend below the treeline, keeping an eye out for a trail on the L to **Le Tour**. When you reach the village, run past the cable car and down the road a little before turning L towards the Le Tour glacier. Pass the Club Alpin Français (CAF) chalet, then as the road ends, turn R down the trail signposted to **Montroc**. Here the 80km route follows the marathon route backwards on the Balcon Nord through Le Planet to **Argentière**.

(11) After Les Chosalets ski lift, turn up L and run a seemingly never-ending series of switchbacks to emerge above the treeline. At the cable car station, turn R and follow the trail to the Chalets de la Pendant and down to **Le Lavancher**, where you follow the reverse marathon route to **Le Bois**.

(12) At the biathlon shooting range in Le Bois, turn L and cross the Arve river on a wooden bridge before turning R. Just before a farm, turn L up a narrow track that ascends steeply. At an intersection with a larger track, turn L towards Le Signal – a buvette overlooking the snout of the Mer de Glace glacier. Turn R and meander up through the moraines via a couple of short ladders.

(13) At a junction turn L onto a path that brings you below the **Montenvers** station. Reach the main path to the glacier and turn R to run through the station and onwards to the hotel building. Behind the hotel is the Glaciorium exhibition building, and to the L of it is the lower track across to the Plan d'Aiguille.

(14) The path is quite exposed in a few sections, so take special care here. At 2071m you meet the Grand Balcon Nord; follow this well-established trail, passing beneath the rock pinnacles of the Aiguilles de Chamonix to your L and eventually reaching the **Plan d'Aiguille** hut at 2200m. This is the last refreshment point on the run.

(15) The path down to Chamonix starts in front of the hut terrace: descend a series of zig-zags and into the forest. Keep going until you reach a path junction at 1437m, then keep R, ignoring a L turn to the Cascade du Dard. Follow signs to the car park for the Aiguille du Midi cable car, and the path emerges suddenly just behind the cable car station. Run past it and straight up the road over the river bridge, then turn R down the high street in **Chamonix**. As you enter the town square, turn L to reach your finish point in front of the town hall.

Route 10
Lac d'Emosson

Start/Finish	SNCF station, Vallorcine (1260m/4133ft)
Distance	12km (7½ miles)
Ascent/Descent	890m (2920ft)
Grade	Trail running, Level 4
Time	3hr 15min
High point	Montagne de Barberine (2100m/6889ft)
Maps	IGN 3630 Chamonix 1:25,000, Rando Editions A1 Pays du Mont Blanc 1:50,000
Public transport	Train/bus to Vallorcine
Season	July to October

This route is a hidden gem and is relatively unfrequented, despite its highlights of seeing the Emosson Dam at very close quarters and traversing the scenic Montagne de Loriaz. There are sudden surprise views to reward you at several points, such as Lac d'Emosson and Mont Ruan from Col du Passet, and the steep drop into the chasm of the Couloir de Barberine.

Safety

This route needs to be completely clear of snow in order to be undertaken safely, due to the risks of slipping above steep drops and of avalanche. The boat prow-shape of the uphill wall of the church at Le Clos in Vallorcine gives you an indication of the level of avalanche protection required historically. Advice on prevailing conditions can be obtained from the Office d'Haute Montagne in Chamonix.

 As you leave the train station, turn R and run past the Vallorcine télécabine, keeping the river on your immediate L. At a bridge, turn sharp L to cross it and continue straight ahead across the road. The path cuts around a chalet garden; on the minor road behind it, turn R along the straight and go past the fortified church and cemetery. In the hamlet of La Mollard the road gives way to a narrow trail that contours into the forest.

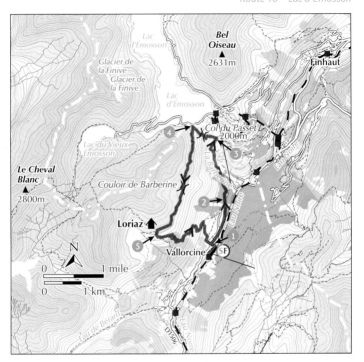

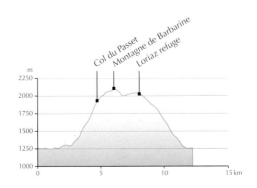

Loriaz and the Barberine mountains

② Follow signs towards the Col du Passet, ignoring a path descending R to the Cascade de Barberine. The trail ascends steadily to 1450m, where it enters a more open section and is rockier underfoot, and then the gradient steepens significantly. There are some rock steps where the odd scrambling move is required before you plunge into the forest again. Note the sign-posts installed by the Swiss, despite just being in France!

③ In the final few hundred metres of ascent towards the **Col du Passet**, the ground becomes a boulder field and you follow a narrow gully up to the pass, stepping carefully over some old winch cables rusting on the ground. As you suddenly arrive on the col, the view ahead makes the effort of the ascent worthwhile. Man-made structures in the mountains are rarely a thing of beauty, but the parabolic curve of the Emosson dam wall, and the glacial blue of the lake, are mesmerising.

Hydration bladders vs water bottles – two is better than one

Rather than carrying just one water receptacle such as a hydration bladder, it's worth having a reserve supply in case the main supply is ruptured or leaks. Bladder systems are highly prone to leaks from loose or split valves and being improperly sealed. Hydration is essential to the performance of a runner, and so taking a second supply is common sense.

(4) Turn sharp L and follow signs for Refuge de Loriaz. You soon encounter a series of metal foot-steps, chains and short steep pitches. The rock is compact and the friction good underfoot, so despite the fixed equipment the route is still very runnable. The trail traverses the Montagne de Loriaz, and after passing the **Couloir de Barberine** it becomes wider and faster. The **Loriaz hut** eventually appears ahead – this can be used as a stop-off for refreshments.

(5) Just below the hut is a metal cross on a huge boulder: the trail turns off L down the hillside just before the cross and plunges into the forest. At the path junction at 1760m, turn L and follow the trails down to **Vallorcine**. Leave the woods at the hamlet of Le Crot and run straight down the road to reach the bridge you crossed at the start of the run. Turn R on the far side to finish back at the station.

Route 11
Col de la Terrasse

Start	SNCF station, Le Buet (1335m/4380ft)
Finish	SNCF station, Finhaut (1224m/4015ft)
Distance	15.3km (9½ miles)
Ascent	1380m (4525ft)
Descent	1490m (4890ft)
Grade	Trail running, Level 4 (and 5km of Skyrunning, Level 4)
Time	4hr 45min
High point	Col de la Terrasse (2640m/8661ft)
Maps	IGN 3630 Chamonix 1:25,000, Rando Editions A1 Pays du Mont Blanc 1:50,000
Public transport	Train/bus to Le Buet, and train from Finhaut
Season	Mid July to early September

This run loops behind the Aiguille du Perron into a remote border region between France and Switzerland. The highlight is the section of Skyrunning above the Loriaz hut, over Col de la Terrasse and down the Gorge de Veudale. To put your efforts into perspective, you'll run where dinosaurs once roamed in the Jurassic era, and will see rocks that still bear their footprints.

Safety

Carry a mobile phone at all times so that you can contact emergency services in the event of an accident. It's worth saving the numbers in your phone before you set off. The Chamonix mountain rescue number is +33 (0)450 531 689. If the weather's mixed, wrap your phone in a drybag or cling film to keep it completely dry.

---

1 Leave the train station car park and turn R along the main road at the Hotel du Buet. Cross the bridge and turn L up the small road to **Le Couteray**. Run around the road corner to the L and then to the R. Continue for a few hundred metres, and just before a farm there's a jeep track off to the L. Follow this, and reach a major corner soon after the initial bend. On the R just after the corner take a small track signposted towards Loriaz.

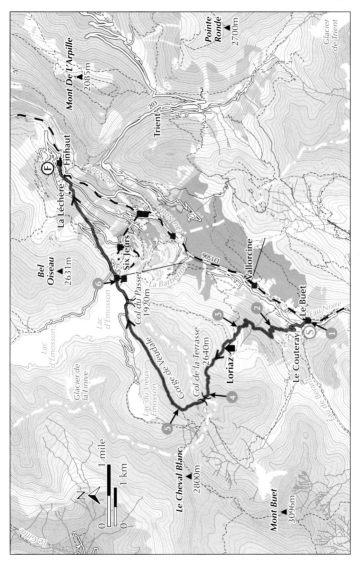

The view down the Gorge de Veudale to Lac d'Emosson

2 At a corner at 1470m, turn L and run up towards the hamlet of Les Granges. As you pass two buildings just below your trail, you meet a large forestry track. Follow this uphill to the R, and at a sharp corner run SA onto a single track, which ascends very gradually at first. As you round a corner the ground becomes steeper, and you cross the Nant de Loriaz bridge. Follow the trail to a junction at 1734m, then turn L up the steeper track.

3 Emerging above the treeline, spot a huge rock with a metal cross on top of it. Beyond it are the farm buildings of the **Refuge de Loriaz**, where you can stop for refreshments and to refill your water bottles. Behind the hut is an amphitheatre of mountains, with the Col de la Terrasse at the head of the deep bowl, and a power line spanning between Le Charmoz and Pointe de la Terrasse. Run up the smaller trail behind the hut, towards the col, and at 2360m it turns slightly L on a rising contour.

4 The ground becomes increasingly steep and rocky, and the final section to the col is an easy scramble. A yellow signpost on **Col de la Terrasse** (2640m) shows you've entered Switzerland. Run almost due N towards the top of the Gorge de Veudale – below you, towards Lac du Vieux Emosson, are enclosures of wire fencing which indicate the location of petrified dinosaur tracks

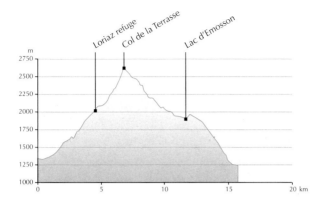

on the rocks, uplifted from an old shoreline. These are well worth a diversion before reaching the top of the **gorge**.

5 The descent is initially quite steep; if there's still snow around you can run and slide down the snow patches, but regulate your speed, as there are rocks lining the edges of the snowfields. The gorge opens out below 2200m and you follow it down to **Lac d'Emosson**. The huge dam wall is up ahead as you round the corner towards **Col du Passet**. Cross the dam on the road, and halfway across look over the edge to see the climbing wall holds that have been fixed to make a route up this vast concrete parabola.

6 Follow the road up to the monorail station and buildings, past **Six Jeurs** and across Gorges des Golettes, and down to 1870m where a trail cuts off to the L towards **La Léchère**. After 600m, cross the road and plunge into the forest again. Turn R at La Léchère to follow a trail S past Vers le Clou. At a path junction at 1380m turn L towards the village, then almost immediately R to reach the road. Follow this down into **Finhaut**, where you finish running at the train station.

Breathing technique at altitude

Experiment with breathing in and out through your nose, both to reduce moisture loss and to control your aerobic output. The nasal passage helps filter the air, and warms it on cold days, so you don't get cold air straight into your lungs.

Route 12
Albert Premier

Start	SNCF station, Le Buet (1335m/4380ft)
Finish	Cable car station, Le Tour (1453m/4767ft)
Distance	15.5km (9¾ miles)
Ascent	1455m (4775ft)
Descent	1305m (4280ft)
Grade	Trail running, Level 3 (with 1km of Level 4)
Time	4hr 15min
High point	Albert Premier refuge (2702m/8864ft)
Maps	IGN 3630 Chamonix 1:25,000, Rando Editions A1 Pays du Mont Blanc 1:50,000
Public transport	Train to Le Buet, and bus from Le Tour
Season	June to September

This trail takes you deep into the heart of the mountains, and its highlight is running the moraine ridge above the Le Tour glacier, with the Aiguille du Chardonnet ahead of you. On the upper trail you're likely to pass mountaineers on their way up to or coming down from the Albert Premier mountain hut, behind which you'll see the peak of the Aiguille du Tour. Take time when you're running to revel in the views, as this route is a photographer's paradise.

Safety

Be aware that on runs such as this, where you're close to the border, your phone may connect to the phone service of one country even though you're in the other. In case of an emergency, you should have several mountain rescue numbers saved in your phone.

---

1 Leave the station platform and turn immediately R down a small lane. Soon on the R there's a tunnel under the track; go through it, and at the path crossroads go SA and over a wooden bridge across the stream. Take the trail SA, which leads via Les Aiguillettes to the Col des Posettes. Take the steeper

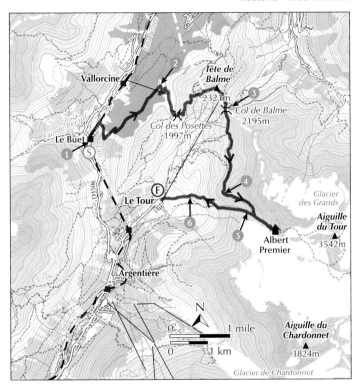

track up the hill, and at 1430m a trail joins from the L. Ahead is a wonderful section of rarely frequented single track; there are a few rocky steps but the trail is very runnable.

2 As you pass beneath the cables of the Télécabine de Vallorcine you soon meet the main track, and turn R to zig-zag up past the upper cable car station. The gradient eases towards the **Col des Posettes**, and it's worth allowing the legs to recover a little. As you reach the col, notice the lines of the Téléski du Plan des Reines coming down the hillside to your L, and below it a trail winding its way up towards the **Tête de Balme**. At 2200m take a trail heading off R towards the Col de Balme, contouring across the hillside.

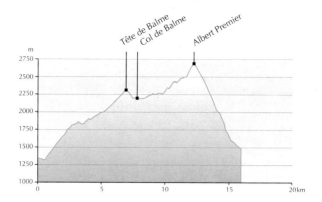

3 The hut on the **Col de Balme** is just in Switzerland, and the refuge guardians have a unique interpretation of customer service, so having put one foot into Swiss territory, continue to contour around to the R and follow the slowly rising trail heading almost due S. It's signposted to the Albert

Running down the lateral moraines of the Glacier du Tour from the Albert Premier hut

Make every step count

With a rocky upper section on this run, the tendency is to throttle back and only use every second or third step to really drive forwards, when your foot is securely braced against a good rock. Try and make every step a positive one in order to gain better momentum; position each step well so that you can push onwards and upwards with every pace.

Premier refuge and runs above the Le Tour ski area. Pass the ephemeral Lac de Charamillon at 2271m, and the path cuts across a slope with an increasing gradient above and below.

4. As you round the corner to the L there's a short, slightly more technical section with fixed equipment across a rocky outcrop. This is soon passed, and ahead lies the final section of the climb. At 2484m the trail reaches a junction at the lateral moraine ridge of the Le Tour glacier; run up this to the **Albert Premier hut**, where refreshments are available. After taking in the panoramic views, return down the moraines to the path junction and this time take the LH path.

5. Run down the wonderful moraine ridge, marvelling as you pass the crumbling snout of the glacier. The smooth rock slabs below are testament to the rate of recent climate change. The kilometre following the viewpoint of the Fenêtre du Tour is the most technical of the route, as you zig-zag down Les Esserins. Be careful here, as your legs will be tired and the ground is steep.

6. The ground suddenly eases off as you cross the Combe de la Vormaine and run across the beginner ski area to reach the village of **Le Tour**. The bus departs from the bridge in front of the cable car station. Take a moment to look back at where you came from, with the snout of the Le Tour glacier far above and the twin summits of the Aiguille du Tour behind.

Route 13
Aiguilles Rouges

Start	SNCF station, Le Buet (1335m/4380ft)
Finish	SNCF station, Servoz (815m/2673ft)
Distance	24.5km (15¼ miles)
Ascent	1410m (4625ft)
Descent	1945m (6380ft)
Grade	Trail running, Level 3 (with 2km of Level 4)
Time	5hr 30min
High point	Col de Salenton (2526m/8287ft)
Maps	IGN 3630 Chamonix 1:25,000, IGN 3530 Samoëns 1:25,000, Rando Editions A1 Pays du Mont Blanc 1:50,000
Public transport	Train/bus to Le Buet, train from Servoz
Season	July to September

This trail explores the wild north side of the Aiguilles Rouges, linking the traditional Alpine villages of Le Buet and Servoz via the high pass of the Col de Salenton. This is a relatively remote run, with considerable altitude gain, but you pass the mountain huts of Pierre à Bérard and Moëde Anterne, as well as the Chalets de Villy, in which you can seek shelter in adverse weather. The scenery is stunning, and you discover a truly different aspect of the Mont Blanc massif. The landscape constantly changes as you pass over the granite of the central massif to the cap of Jurassic limestones and shales of the Salenton. There are no opt-outs or shortcuts on this trail, but this level of commitment may be an attraction to some.

1 From the station at Le Buet, cross the car park and road to reach the nature reserve information board and take the trail signposted to the Cascade de Bérard. Follow the recently installed metal walkways to see the main cascade below the café. The trail follows the L bank of the river to the La Vordette bridge at 1528m, where you cross onto the R bank and soon emerge above the treeline into the upper Bérard valley.

Safety

Be wary of tackling this route too early in the season, as snow patches often remain on both sides of the Col de Salenton until July. You can get information about the prevailing conditions by visiting the Office d'Haute Montagne in the Maison de la Montagne, next to the church in Chamonix, or by calling the Refuge de la Pierre à Bérard (+33 (0)450 546 208) or the Refuge de Moëde Anterne (+33 (0)450 936 043). If you decide to risk the snow patches, setting off in the late morning or afternoon should allow the snow sufficient time to soften and therefore be easier to run on.

2 Follow the upper trail to the **Pierre à Bérard mountain hut**, which is built into the lee of a huge boulder to protect it from being destroyed by avalanches in winter. In the summer months the hut is a delightful place to stop for food and drinks. Just behind the hut to the R is a water trough where you can wash and refill your water bottles before continuing. Note that there is no access to clean water for the next couple of hours.

The pretty Refuge Pierre à Bérard hut

3 Next to the water trough is a sign for the Col de Salenton. Initially the trail is obvious, following a series of zig-zags up the hillside, then as you pass out of sight of the hut and cross a boulder field the terrain becomes more technical. If you're using poles, be sure to take your hands out of the wrist loops so that you can use your hands on the rocks, and to protect your wrists in event of a fall.

4 The route is marked with red paint spots on the rocks; notice the colour of the rock changing beneath your feet from the warm red of granite to the white of limestone and the black of shales. Above and to the L, the Col de Salenton comes into view, marked by a large cairn. The trail traverses over steeper loose ground to reach the **pass**. If you're running this route early in the season, expect to cross a few snow patches here. Given the remoteness of the route from this point, if you're feeling especially fatigued it's best to turn around and return to Le Buet.

5 On the far side of the pass the valley opens out before you, and you're rewarded for your efforts with a stunning panorama, dominated by the Rochers des Fiz. Descend quickly over the scree, and just after the limestone cliffs to your R, turn R and bend around the hillside to zig-zag down towards some high grazing pastures. On the far side of these is a stream crossing, which can usually be done keeping dry feet by hopping from stone to stone.

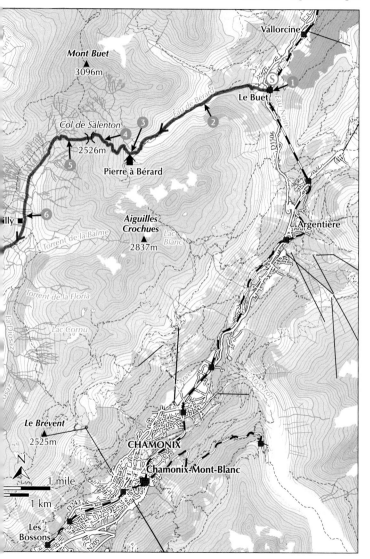

Crossing the Col de Salenton

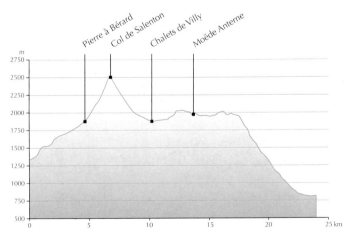

Getting a grip

If you encounter snow patches, you can help safeguard a traverse on steeper sections by placing a running pole just below where you wish to place your downhill foot. You can then brace your running shoe against the pole to stop it sliding downhill. When running on granite such as the slabs before Col de Salenton, trust the grip on your trail shoes as it offers great friction. On the shales on the far side of the pass, be less trusting of grip but use the cushioning effect of the softer screes to allow for a fast descent.

6 In front of you are the farm buildings of the **Chalets de Villy**, where you can replenish your water bottles in the trough. Ahead the trail ascends gently, and the path widens as you approach the **Moëde Anterne** mountain hut. There are great views to the L across to Brévent and the whole Mont Blanc massif. Hot food and refreshments can be obtained at the hut, and behind it is a water gauge from where you follow the signpost to the Lac de Pormenaz.

7 The trail undulates around the lake before dipping to reach the **Chalets de Pormenaz**. Here it curves around the mountainside and drops more steeply down towards Servoz. The end is in sight below, but track is quite technical in places so you need to maintain concentration.

8 Follow signs for Servoz as you pass through **La Fontaine** and **Le Bouchet**. Enter **Servoz** and run through the village centre until you reach a mini-roundabout. Turn L down the long straight road and follow it for the final kilometre to reach the SNCF train station.

Route 14
Mont Buet

Start/Finish	SNCF station, Le Buet (1335m/4380ft)
Distance	18km (11 miles)
Ascent/Descent	1775m (5825ft)
Grade	Trail running, Level 4 (with 4km of Skyrunning, Level 3)
Time	5hr 30min
High point	Mont Buet (3096m/10,157ft)
Maps	IGN 3630 Chamonix 1:25,000, Rando Editions A1 Pays du Mont Blanc 1:50,000
Public transport	Train/bus to and from Le Buet
Season	Mid July to September

This route offers a real challenge as you run to the highest trekking summit in the Mont Blanc massif. The peak is largely non-technical, although you'll encounter a lot of rough ground where route-finding skills are essential. You're rewarded with an unparalleled panoramic vantage point with superb views of the glaciers, from Le Tour to Argentière, Mer de Glace and Les Bossons. If you're a runner who has no aspirations as a mountaineer, this summit view is one of the best in the Alps.

Mont Buet is nicknamed 'Mont Blanc des Dames' (the ladies' Mont Blanc), as in Victorian times it was common practice for women to ascend Mont Buet, while the men climbed Mont Blanc. Nowadays it's a common acclimatisation peak for both sexes to ascend before climbing Mont Blanc, and it's a wild paradise for trail running. This route has a significant section classified as Skyrunning due to the terrain and altitude.

1 Follow the track for Route 13 until you reach the **Pierre à Bérard** mountain hut. You can purchase snacks here to fuel up for the next 1200m of ascent, and you can refill your water bottles in the trough behind the hut. (This is often the last drinkable running water that you'll encounter until you return to this point, so be sure to carry plenty.) Next to the water trough is a signpost pointing in the direction of the Col de Salenton; the trail initially gains height up a series of zig-zags, with the terrain becoming rougher as you climb.

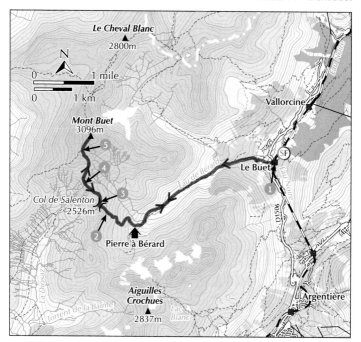

Safety

This route is one of the few 'out-and-back' routes in the guidebook; you can opt out at any stage and return the way you came. It's important to assess whether there's too much snow on the mountain before embarking, and to be confident of your navigation skills in poor visibility. Significant snow patches often remain between the Col de Salenton and the summit of Mont Buet until late August. Before you set off, obtain information about the conditions from the Office d'Haute Montagne in the Maison de la Montagne next to the church in Chamonix, or by calling the Refuge de la Pierre à Bérard (+33 (0)450 546 208). If snows remain, setting off in the mid-morning allows time for those making an Alpine start from the hut to have kicked steps in any fresh snow, and it should allow the snow patches enough time to soften so they can be run on without sliding too much. Note that the summit of Mont Buet has near-permanent snow cover.

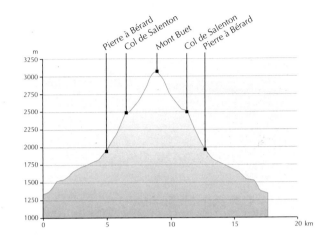

(2) As you pass over the ridgeline and lose sight of the Pierre à Bérard hut behind you, the trail soon gives way to bare rock slabs. Keep an eye out for red dots of paint on the rocks marking the way – follow these rather than the myriad of cairns that have sprung up, often misleadingly, in this area of the mountain. The granite rock provides great traction for running, and you can ascend quickly over this section.

(3) Soon the rock gives way to boulders and the route-finding becomes a little more difficult, but the red dots lead you through the path of least resistance. Ahead to the L is the **Col de Salenton**, but don't be tempted to gain too much height towards it, as you traverse nearly 100m below its cairn, past the crags of the Aiguille de Salenton. In front of you Mont Buet comes fully into sight, and far ahead to the L edge of the summit ridge is a mountain rescue radio relay transmitter with solar panels, which is a useful waypoint.

(4) Once you've passed the Aiguille de Salenton, the trail follows a rising traverse around the bowl of the mountain to reach a small plateau at 2650m. Here it's worth stopping for a breather and to take in the view of the Mont Blanc massif, which will just have come into view for the first time. The trail turns R behind a small ridgeline, and ahead is the crest leading straight up to

Mont Blanc from the summit of Mont Buet

the radio relay. Once you gain this ridge the gradient increases significantly, and it's essential to pace yourself well in order to maintain momentum.

5   Just below the radio relay is a cairn, at the lower end of the Arête de la Mortine, and the trail turns sharply R to regain the ridge after 100m. The summit of **Mont Buet** is ahead, marked by a large square cairn with a small cross on top. As you reach the summit be very wary not to continue on any snow patches beyond the cairn, as they are unsupported cornices overhanging the NW face and are highly unstable. A small triangulation point about 20m to the SE of the cairn marks the true summit at 3109m. On a clear day you can see the Jura mountains to the N, the Matterhorn to the E, and the Mont Blanc massif to the S.

Descending scree

On the scree of the upper mountain, keep your weight forward when descending, as this will lessen chances of a slip and allow you to use gravity to your advantage, rather than using muscular energy to brake.

Descent from Buet to Col de Salenton

Descend by exactly the same route that you ascended, remembering to refill with water at the Pierre à Bérard hut on the way down. Below the hut, follow the obvious trail back down the Bérard valley, and after crossing the first bridge keep a lookout for a good place to take a dip or an ice bath in the river, as there are many delightful pools to wash off the dust and dirt, and to help the legs recover.

There's a train every hour from **Le Buet** back to Chamonix, so if you've just missed one, stop off for a drink at the historic Hotel Le Buet on the corner of the road opposite the station platform.

Route 15
Le Brévent

Start	SNCF station, Les Houches (970m/3182ft)
Finish	Cable car station, Brévent summit (2525m/8284ft)
Distance	12.3km (7¾ miles)
Ascent	1620m (5315ft)
Descent	125m (410ft)
Grade	Trail running, Level 3
Time	4hr 15min
High point	Brévent (2525m/8284ft)
Maps	IGN 3531 St Gervais 1:25,000, Rando Editions A1 Pays du Mont Blanc 1:50,000
Public transport	Train to Les Houches SNCF
Season	June to September
Note	This is an arid area and you can't rely on running water to top up your bottles. Make sure you set off with at least 1.5L.

Looking at the route profile, you'd be excused for thinking this is a long uphill slog. Far from it: this route offers a great range of terrain, different views at each turn, and a wonderful progression of ecosystems as you gain altitude.

1 Leave the train station and turn L onto the road, which crosses back up over the railway line. Almost immediately on the L is a steep track leading up into the woods. Follow it upwards, then cross the road and continue on a track on the far side. Soon after, at a path junction, turn L to cross the road again and run up the path ahead. The next kilometre of trail curves around the hill of Les Crêts.

Safety

Beware of running this route out of the suggested season, for two reasons: the cable car down from Brévent will be closed, and the remaining or early snows on the slopes leading up to Le Brévent can conceal holes between the boulders in which it's easy to injure an ankle.

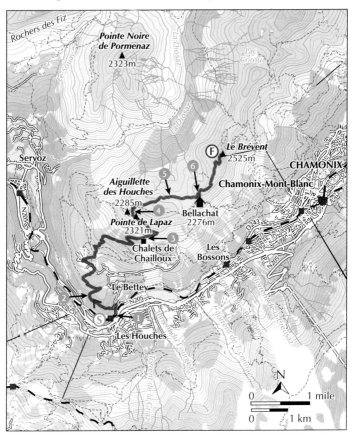

2 At a path junction at 1190m, turn sharp L towards Morand, and then a couple of minutes beyond the chalets, take the R turn towards **Le Bettey**. On reaching the road, turn L and run past the car park. Keep an eye out for a signpost on the R towards Le Plan de la Cry; here take the upper trail towards Chalets de Chailloux.

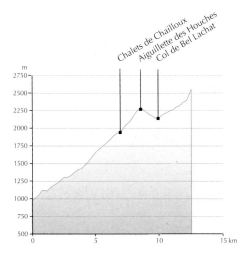

(3) Break out of the treeline at 1900m and almost immediately arrive at the farm buildings of **Chailloux**. The trail continues for a couple of hundred metres beyond the chalets, then the route doubles back on itself and traverses below the ridgeline of **Pointe de Lapaz** on your R.

(4) The path steepens and zig-zags at an increasing gradient up to the **Aiguillette des Houches**. Fortunately the climb is soon over, and as you reach the ridge crest the views ahead to the Rochers des Fiz are contrasting and beautiful. The mountains take on a different shape from the needles of the Mont Blanc massif.

(5) After the height gain, you're rewarded with a slightly descending traverse across the Col de Bel Lachat. The glacially scoured terrain is peppered with marshy areas and small ponds. Ahead is Brévent, with the cable car station perched on its rocky summit, seemingly defying gravity.

(6) The path starts to ascend again and you'll see the roof of the **Bellachat hut** below you to the R as you run past. Follow the path up towards Brévent, and the trail becomes increasingly rocky underfoot. Just after an exposed switchback that's protected with a safety handrail, there's a delightful section of trail over smooth rock slabs.

Dress for the aspect

Always look at the route on a map and study the slope aspects you intend to run. In the Alps in summer, east-facing mountainsides will catch the morning light and heat up first; southerly slopes will get most sun generally in the afternoon; westerly slopes are cool in the morning and warm in the afternoon, and northerly slopes are cool throughout. Plan your clothing and hydration accordingly.

Dabs of paint on rocks lead the way, and don't forget to savour the views behind you towards Mont Blanc. Reach a signpost just below the summit of **Le Brévent**, and turn sharp R to ascend the rocky trail to the cable car station. It's recommended that you catch the cable car down from here to save your legs, but keen souls could run down the ski run track to Planpraz and get the télécabine from there.

Rocky singletrack trail near Le Brévent

Route 16
Le Prarion

Start/Finish	Bellevue cable car, Les Houches (993m/3257ft)
Distance	19.8km (12¼ miles)
Ascent/Descent	1340m (4395ft)
Grade	Trail running, Level 2 (with 1km of Level 3)
Time	5hrs
High point	Le Prarion (1969m/6460ft)
Maps	IGN 3531 St Gervais 1:25,000, Rando Editions A1 Pays du Mont Blanc 1:50,000
Public transport	Train to Les Houches, bus to Bellevue
Season	June to October
Note	You're likely to encounter farm livestock on this run, especially in the area from La Charme to Le Prarion. Be especially careful in selecting water sources in areas where animals are grazing. It's worth refilling your water bottles before leaving Bionnassay village at one of the stone water troughs.

This run is interesting for the local history, and for the impressive view right up the Chamonix valley from the top of Le Prarion. You run across the Kandahar ski piste, which is famed for hosting ski World Cup events since 1937, through the village of Bionnassay, which was catastrophically flooded in 1892 with 175 lives lost when a sub-glacial water pocket burst in the Tête Rousse glacier, and across the Tramway du Mont Blanc, which opened in 1907 and is the highest railway in France.

Safety

The summit ridge of Le Prarion is safe, but don't be tempted to venture off the track as there are major drops, especially on the east-facing slopes. Also be very careful descending the north ridge during or after rain, as the trail is exposed and slippery. If running this route in poor weather, you're advised to return from La Charme to Col de Voza and run down the route you ascended.

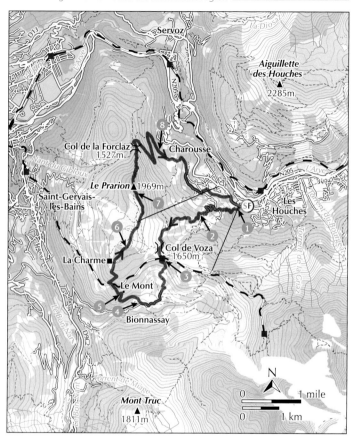

The Tour du Mont Blanc

The first half of this route is shared with the Tour du Mont Blanc trek, so you can follow the TMB signposts as it's exceptionally well marked. Be aware that trekkers on the route will be moving slowly in comparison to you, often with exceptionally large rucksacks, so try to give them a wide berth as they're unable to change direction as quickly as you are.

1 At the far end of the cable car station car park, take the stairs leading up to a small ski lift, which is closed in the summer months. Turn R, and soon reach a large track, where you turn L uphill through the forest. Climb steeply, and emerge from the trees close to some chalets.

The track runs past the buildings; veer R at the road, then at the next junction veer L towards Maison Neuve. Run up a series of switchbacks on the road, and at the cable car station turn R to reach the stony jeep track behind the buildings, and follow the signs to the Col de Voza.

2 Run past a series of mountain restaurants, including the charming Vieilles Luges, situated next to the trail, and ascend in a series of steeper pitches and flatter sections. The route takes you through the heart of the Les Houches ski area, and you can see vividly the environmental impact of piste skiing.

Keep following the signs for the Col de Voza and you finally see the hotel building, then descend for the last hundred metres or so towards the **pass**. Run across the Tramway du Mont Blanc railway tracks and plunge down the track into the forest on the far side.

3 Take a quick moment to appreciate the view of the shown face of the Aiguille du Bionnassay ahead of you, and the foreboding Aiguille du Goûter to your L. Run steeply downhill, then as the woods soon give way to alpages, run through a series of charming traditional hamlets and farms. As you approach the valley floor the stony track turns to tarmac; follow the road into **Bionnassay** village, which remains very traditionally French with no sign of being altered in the slightest by tourism.

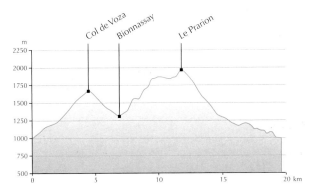

111

Ascending above the farm at La Charme

4 Just after the village, at 1314m, a farm track turns off R. Run along this and follow it as it curves around to the L, gaining height steadily. After nearly a kilometre the trail turns R and goes steeply uphill towards a farm building. Just before you reach it, turn R up the track to the buildings at Le Mont. You've now left the TMB behind and you're running on the Tour du Pays du Mont Blanc, so you'll occasionally see the 'TPMB' on signposts.

5 Turn L before **Le Mont** and run the faint trail through the woods and a beautiful clearing, before crossing the Tramway du Mont Blanc again and ascending more steeply into the forests on the far side. Watch for a sharp LH turnoff at 1715m, then after a couple of hundred metres turn R to run up into the clearing and up the field to reach the farm at **La Charme**. Cross the main farm track and continue upwards.

6 Pass through a forest section before emerging into the upper Les Houches ski area again. Keep running along the higher ground, close to the top of all the Téléski installations, and soon reach the Hôtel du Prarion. You can buy refreshments here, and just behind it is the Le Prarion cable car station. To

Viewing table on the summit of Le Prarion

the L of this is the start of the trail to Le Prarion, which meanders through the woods, clearings and small rocky steps to gain the ridgeline.

7 As you near the summit of **Le Prarion** the ground becomes more exposed, and at the top there's an orientation table. Enjoy the views along the length of the valley and up towards Mont Blanc, then run onwards to start a steep and quite technical descent towards Col de la Forclaz. The single track is frequently disrupted by tree roots and rocky sections, so watch your footing.

8 At the **col**, turn R and more zig-zags bring you down to a forest road. Run along this until you reach a sharp L corner, then run SA and climb gently to Charousse, whose traditional farm buildings have graced many a calendar and Christmas card. Continue onwards, and the trail emerges in Les Chavants. When you reach the road, follow it to a corner where the cables of the Prarion cable car are above your head.

Run ahead at a road junction to the village of Le Crêt, and just after the gîte look for a path off down to the L, which brings you out on the road. Turn R to return to the Bellevue cable car, and just before you reach it the road passes through a tunnel under the ski piste. The bus stop is on the R in front of the cable car.

Route 17
Col de Tricot

Start	Town hall, Les Houches (1010m/3313ft)
Finish	Tourist office, Les Contamines (1167m/3828ft)
Distance	15.5km (9¾ miles)
Ascent	1400m (4595ft)
Descent	1245m (4085ft)
Grade	Trail running, Level 3 (Level 2 from Chalets du Truc)
Time	4hr 15min
High point	Col de Tricot (2120m/6955ft)
Maps	IGN 3531 St Gervais 1:25,000, Rando Editions A1 Pays du Mont Blanc 1:50,000
Public transport	Bus/train to Les Houches; bus from Contamines to Le Fayet and then train to Chamonix
Season	July to September
Note	When crossing the suspension bridge over the Torrent de Miage, walk to avoid it shaking excessively and only have two people on it at a time.

This run starts and ends in bustling Alpine villages, but the middle section is one of the wildest landscapes, with a real sense of adventure thrown in. You cross a Himalayan-style wire suspension footbridge and a steep high pass, and you discover remote mountain huts. This is a taste of a truly traditional part of France, in great, unspoilt scenery.

Safety

Don't try and run across the Col de Tricot if there's snow remaining on the far side, as a slide there would have very serious consequences. For this reason, the suggested running season is from July onwards and not before. As the Tricot is on a variant of the Tour du Mont Blanc, you'll be able to get information on current conditions from the Office de Haute Montagne in Chamonix.

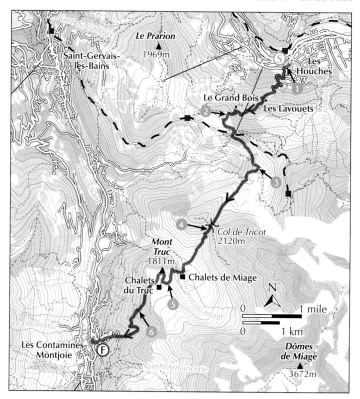

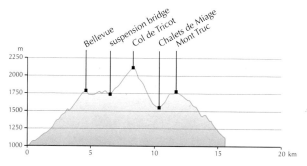

> ## Mud in the mountains
>
> This route is muddier underfoot than some of the trails on the granite of the main Chamonix valley, so if you've got a choice of footwear, take some with a good tread for grip. You'll appreciate this on the ascent to Bellevue top station, and on the descent from Tricot.

1 From Les Houches town hall, head towards the base station of the Bellevue cable car. After less than 200m the road crosses a stream; on the far side turn sharp L up the road leading up the hill. Ignore the turnoffs and follow the switchbacks upwards to reach **Les Lavouets** at 1270m.

    The road turns into a muddy trail as it enters the woods, and there's a very runnable section up to the path junction at **Le Grand Bois** at 1440m. Take the track off L, heading up the hill, where the going gets steeper and more technical.

2 You suddenly burst out of the trees at the bottom of a Téléski. Follow the trails up to the Bellevue top station, which is obvious on the skyline ahead. As you reach it, run across to the Tramway du Mont Blanc platform, and just on the far side of the tracks is the start of your trail. Head L and run in a SE direction. There are a few steep and exposed sections, often protected with fixed equipment, but these are short.

Reaching the Tramway du Mont Blanc

③ Follow signs for the Col de Tricot, and at 1780m turn R and drop down to reach the suspension bridge spanning the meltwater river from the base of the Bionnassay glacier. Cross the bridge with care, and on the far side turn L at a path junction up towards the Tricot pass.

Crossing the suspension bridge

The upper Tricot valley opens out as you climb above the treeline. The path is eroded and braided, but eventually the **col** at 2120m comes into view. The descent on the far side is steep and zig-zags over rough ground, so be careful with your footwork here. Far below you can see the **Chalets de Miage** at 1559m.

④ As you descend, the path becomes easier underfoot, and you're able to run fast. You can top up your water bottles at the chalets in the water trough, and you can buy refreshments at the Refuge de Miage. On the far side of the main river, turn off L up the hillside, signposted for the Chalets du Truc.

⑤ This is your last ascent of the day, and there's only a couple of hundred metres of climbing, so keep pushing onwards until you reach the top. Here you can veer off R from the main path to take in the top of **Mont Truc** (1811m). It may be a tiny summit, but the views across to the Aiguille de Bionnassay and Dômes du Miage are stupendous. Run down to the **Chalets du Truc**, which are obvious below you, and pick up the jeep track descending into the woods towards Les Contamines. Enjoy the next kilometre of running, as it's easy and fast.

⑥ Just after the first switchback there's a turn off to the L along a great single-track section through the forest. It merges back onto the main track lower down, and this is followed to reach **Les Contamines**.

At the road head is a car park; you can avoid all the road switchbacks by taking a signposted path that cuts between buildings in a direct line down to the village centre. Finish on the main road near the tourist office and church.

Route 18
Lac Vert

Start	SNCF station, Servoz (815m/2673ft)
Finish	Town square, Chedde (598m/1962ft)
Distance	12.6km (7¾ miles)
Ascent	560m (1835ft)
Descent	775m (2540ft)
Grade	Trail running, Level 1
Time	2hr 45min
High point	Plaine Joux (1350m/4429ft)
Maps	IGN 3530 Samoëns 1:25,000, Rando Editions A1 Pays du Mont Blanc 1:50,000
Public transport	Bus/train to Servoz, train from Chedde
Season	March to December

If you like running in the woods and want a change from the spruce and larch of Chamonix valley, this route introduces you to a nice variety of mature forest. It's a great option for early or late season, or if there's bad weather in the mountains and the snowline is dropping. In autumn it can be a delight, with the leaves of the deciduous trees turning orange. Of historical note, you'll run past the old Sancollemoz Sanatorium at Plateau d'Assy, where Marie Curie died in 1934 of pernicious anaemia, which she had developed over years of exposure to radiation through her research.

① Exit the station at Servoz and follow the long straight road towards the village. After crossing a bridge, turn L on the far side and drop onto the track alongside the river, and then follow it until you reach another bridge. Here turn R away from the river, and you'll enter Vieux Servoz. Cross the road and continue up through the village.

② The path ascends into the woods and is well signposted as you're on a variant of the Tour du Pays du Mont Blanc hiking trail. Follow signs upwards to **La Cote**, where you pass through a small car park at a road head, and then towards Lac Vert. Beyond La Cote the path gets steeper as it climbs up through the woods on long switchbacks.

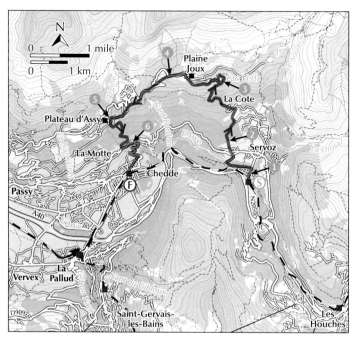

Safety

This route is often possible throughout the year as it follows tracked easy snowshoe trails in winter, but beware of skiers at Plaine Joux who may not be used to dodging runners.

---

3 You emerge at **Lac Vert** just below a chalet café, where you can get refreshments. The route's highlight is the looping run around this pretty mountain lake, which lives up to its name and is emerald green in colour. Run anticlockwise around the lake and you'll hit a small road on the SW corner; turn R and follow it up until you spot a signpost on the L for a trail to Plaine Joux.

This path emerges from the forest just below the ski lifts at **Plaine Joux** and you contour across to the L of all the buildings. The views across to the Mont Blanc massif and Mont Joly are stunning; you'll soon lose them in the forests, so take a moment to savour them.

The emerald-coloured Lac Vert

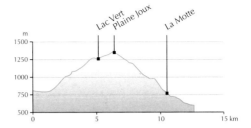

4. Continue running, keeping the road on your R, and the path develops into a great trail, which soon dips L away from the road and down into the woods. Cross a road that descends from the R and plunge into the woods again. When you hit the road again, follow it for a few hundred metres around a gully until you spot a path off L on the hairpin. Drop steeply down, and there's a great single track towards **Plateau d'Assy**. Just before you reach the village, cross a road before taking a short track to meet the road again.

5. Follow the road past the old Sancellemoz Sanatorium, then turn sharp L just before the stream. This trail leads you through spectacular woodland and clearings down to a path junction at 790m. Head R, and after crossing the stone bridge, turn L into **La Motte**. On the road, turn L and continue until you reach a R exit to Les Soudans.

6. Simply follow the road through wide sweeping turns down to Chedde, passing a spectacular waterfall next to the road. As you enter **Chedde**, turn down Route du Lac Vert, which brings you into the town square just around the corner from the station.

The importance of tape

Always carry a roll of elasticated sticky medical tape such as zinc oxide, which you can use as strapping tape in the event of a turned ankle or to support a knee, and to hold a dressing firmly in place on a cut. Tape can also be used to repair a broken running pole, hold a dying running shoe together, or to secure clothing or pack straps that are blowing into your face.

Route 19
Charousse

Start	Bellevue cable car, Les Houches (993m/3257ft)
Finish	SNCF station, Servoz (815m/2673ft)
Distance	8km (5 miles)
Ascent	330m (1080ft)
Descent	520m (1705ft)
Grade	Trail running, Level 1 (with 1km of Level 2)
Time	1hr 30min
High point	Charousse (1210m/3969ft)
Maps	IGN 3531 St Gervais 1:25,000, Rando Editions A1 Pays du Mont Blanc 1:50,000
Public transport	Bus to Bellevue, train from Servoz
Season	May to November

This is one of the easiest and shortest trail runs in this guidebook – ideal for a few hours' free time, or in the early morning or evening. It explores the traditional, less commercial end of the valley, and you run through beautiful mature mixed woodland.

Safety

Objectively this route is very safe and can be run in all weathers apart from lightning storms.

---

1 With your back to the Bellevue cable car, turn L and run along the road through the tunnel under the ski piste. Immediately cross a stream, then as the road curves R and then L, look for a signposted path off to the L towards Les Crêts. Run up the hillside to reach a small road

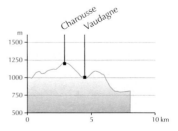

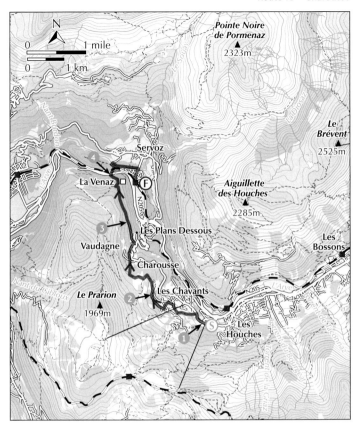

next to the old gîte, and follow this to the corner of a larger road where you veer L upwards. This takes you to **Les Chavants**, and you'll see a signpost indicating that you're on the Tour du Pays du Mont Blanc, and onwards to Charousse.

2 The road ends at La Côte; follow the bridleway around the corner past the farm buildings of **Charousse**. Enter the forests just after the alpage clearing and descend to a path junction at 1170m, then turn R and run downwards alongside the stream to reach **Vaudagne** village.

Charousse chalet buildings and alpage

At the road, continue SA down into the centre, towards the small church. As the road turns sharp R there's a footpath cutting off at the corner, which leads down to a T-junction on the road, where you turn L and follow the road to its end at the parking area just beyond **Les Plans Dessous**.

3 The road gives way to a nice section of trail through the woods, and you run along the traverse for just over a kilometre until a path descends in from the L. Turn R and drop steeply downhill past the ruins of **La Venaz**, and zig-zag down through the deciduous forest, arriving above the main road to Chamonix.

4 The trail crosses above the road tunnel entrance, and on the far side you reach a small track. Follow this down L and cross a bridge over the Arve river. On the far bank, immediately turn R and run along the small river path. After a kilometre you reach the Pont de l'Avenue bridge. Cut up R over it, and the **Servoz** train station is just ahead on the L at the end of the straight.

Trip hazards

Tree roots may be the bane of a runner's life, and the cause of many a turned ankle or fall, but try to use them positively and adapt your foot placement on ascents to brace against roots for traction and support. On descents, try to avoid landing on roots, as they're often slippery and present a clear trip hazard. If in doubt, don't be afraid to slow down.

Route 20
Nid d'Aigle

Start	SNCF station, Le Fayet (580m/1902ft)
Finish	Tramway du Mont Blanc terminus, Nid d'Aigle (2372m/7782ft)
Distance	20.4km (12¾ miles)
Ascent	1695m (5560ft)
Descent	100m (330ft)
Grade	Trail running, Level 3
Time	3hr 30min
High point	Nid d'Aigle (2372m/7782ft)
Maps	IGN 3531 St Gervais 1:25,000, Rando Editions A1 Pays du Mont Blanc 1:50,000
Public transport	Train to Le Fayet and from Nid d'Aigle
Season	July to September

This run closely follows the route of the famous Montée du Nid d'Aigle trail race, which ascends all the way from the valley floor in Le Fayet into high the mountains at the Nid d'Aigle. You finish at the mountain railway station, where mountaineers head upwards on their ascent of Mont Blanc, yet this route requires no mountain techniques and is a running route. It involves a height gain of over 1600m, but there are several easier flatter sections where you can recuperate.

1 Run up the road in front of the station and you'll see the rails of the Tramway du Mont Blanc following the road for a short while. Follow them, and turn R into the Parc Thermal on the corner. Run through the park on the lower road, and at the end where it doubles back on itself, continue on the paths that take you past the waterfall and then to Le Chatelet. Here, on race day, there's a loop back around into the centre of **St Gervais** and an aid station. It's well worth running through the town to see its well-preserved old buildings.

2 From the town centre, follow the main road up the valley, and at the small roundabout to Les Contamines take the exit R and run down towards the bridge. Before crossing it, turn L through a car park and onto the trails. This

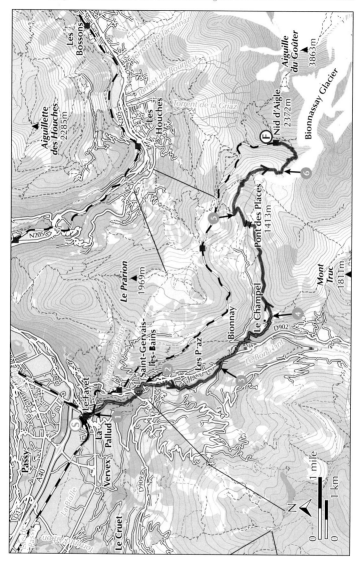

Safety

Don't be tempted to undertake this route if there is any snow remaining on the upper sections, as the steeper ground below the Nid d'Aigle would be unsafe in trainers. A good indication of route safety is whether the Tramway du Mont Blanc train is open all the way to Nid d'Aigle, and is operating.

track is called the 'Promenade du Mont Blanc', and it soon reaches **Les Praz**, where you cross the river bridge to continue the trail on the far bank.

3 Follow the track until the power lines ahead indicate you've arrived at the electricity station. Here turn L across the bridge, and when you reach the main road, turn R. Arriving in **Bionnay**, turn L up through the village, and soon after crossing the bridge of the Torrent de Bionnassay, take the L turn up towards **Le Champel**.

4 Continue along the road, which you share with the Tour du Mont Blanc, until it veers L to cross the river at the **Pont des Places** (1413m). On the far side turn R up to Sur les Maures and curve back L to gain height and reach a group of buildings at 1495m, where the power lines change direction overhead.

5 After the buildings at 1557m, the farm track becomes a path and the scenery opens out as you leave the forests behind. Near the Chalet de l'Are, ignore

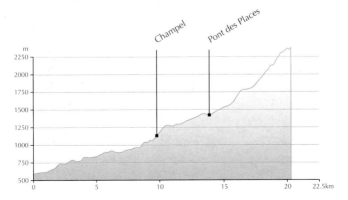

127

Ibex on a rock just below the Nid d'Aigle

the R turn to the suspension bridge and the Col de Tricot, and instead take the path closest to the **Bionnassay glacier**. Enjoy running the flatter section here, as it provides a brief reprieve before the final steep climb.

6 At the far end of the plateau the path zig-zags steeply upwards, before a rising traverse below a rock band. There's a short section of ladders up through the rock step, and then the route weaves upwards through the boulder-strewn hillside. The icefall of the Bionnassay glacier is stunning below, and in your vertical quest, don't forget to take a moment to revel in the views behind you.

Ahead is the finish line at the **Nid d'Aigle** – the terminus of the Tramway du Mont Blanc. Here you can catch the train down, to arrive next to the SNCF station in Le Fayet.

Temperature drop during big alpine ascents

This route entails a significant altitude gain: you start in the low valley, where peak summer temperatures are around 35°C, and finish close to glaciers where you'll be cooled by the katabatic mountain breezes. Don't be fooled into assuming you'll remain warm enough throughout – carry a warmer layer for the upper section, or the descent.

Route 21
Refuge de Doran

Start/Finish	Plan Chevalier car park (816m/2677ft)
Distance	11.9km (7½ miles); from Sallanches: 18.9km (11¾ miles)
Ascent/Descent	995m (3265ft)
Grade	Trail running, Level 2 (with 3km of Level 3)
Time	3hrs; from Sallanches: 4hr 30min
High point	Arête des Saix (1840m/6036ft)
Maps	IGN 3430 La Clusaz-Grand Bornand 1:25,000, Rando Editions A1 Pays du Mont Blanc 1:50,000
Public transport	Train or bus to Sallanches
Season	May to November

This run is a great introduction to the Aravis chain of mountains, which offer great views of the western aspect of the Mont Blanc massif. While the glittering summit of Mont Blanc may be the highest peak in the Alps, it's the might of the jagged peak of Pointe Percée above you that catches your eye on these trails. While running in the Aravis you'll enjoy a region largely unspoiled by tourism, and get a glimpse of rural alpage living and farming.

There is no public transport to Plan Chevalier, but the following description includes an alternative start from Sallanches, adding 3.5km of road running to the start and end of the route and 1hr 30mins to the total time for the route.

Safety

Be aware of the *patous* mountain dogs protecting flocks of sheep during the summer months. Dog owners are advised not to take their pets running with them in this region, especially in the height of summer. Also be aware that in early season there could be remaining snow patches near the Arête des Saix, in which case an alternative run should be considered. To check conditions, call the Refuge du Doran on +33 (0)450 580 800, or Mayères on +33 (0)450 782 928.

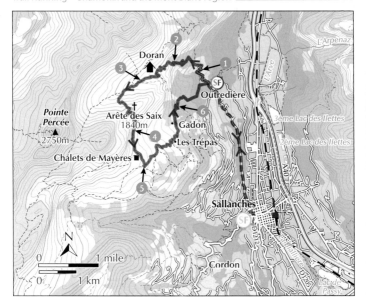

Alternative start from Sallanches

Those travelling by public transport should start running in front of the town hall in Sallanches. Keep the river to your L, and run upstream until you can turn off R to follow Rue Saint-Joseph. After crossing the Ruisseau de Bellegarde, turn L onto Route de la Provence. Follow this SA up the hillside; the road becomes Route d'Outrediere and you reach the Plan Chevalier car park.

1 From the car park just beyond the corner of the road, follow the small road up to the hamlet of **Outredière**. At the far end of the village, behind the last chalets, is a path off to the L. Run up this, on the trail signed with the letter 'Z'. At the first path junction ignore the path off to the R, which leads to the climbing crag of La Pierre à Voix, and continue ahead on the forest track.

2 The path ascends a series of switchbacks as you work your way up through the forest to below the cliffs of the Saix Noirs. Cross an ephemeral streambed on the fourth bend, before rounding the corner and ascending steeply to the R of a huge boulder on the hillside. Here you gain height quickly, crossing some complicated terrain where the hillside has eroded

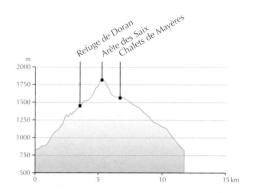

into a braiding of small valleys and larger ravines. The path contours in and out of each one as it traverses up the hillside.

As you run upwards you cross three streams before reaching the bridge over the Dière torrent at 1350m. On the far bank of the river, continue steeply up the forest trail and out of the treeline, and soon reach a path junction where you bear R to reach the **Refuge du Doran** at 1495m. You can obtain refreshments here throughout the advised season for this running route, and above the refuge is an amazing view of Pointe Percée – the highest peak in the Aravis mountain chain.

3 Leave the cluster of buildings behind you and head up into the Doran valley. At the path junction 200m beyond the hut, turn L and run with the stream on your R. At another path junction at 1560m, turn L again towards the Chalets de Mayères. The path steepens and you ascend a series of switchbacks to arrive at the **Arête des Saix** (1840m), which is marked by a cross. After taking in the view, start the descent, keeping L at another path junction to traverse across the hillside.

4 Run down the trail, which bends R at two pine trees, and come to a short section of steeper ground where you might need to use your hands from time to time as it's briefly quite exposed. At the foot of the steeper section the trail leads SA to the **Chalet des Mayères**, where you can get refreshments. To your R is a small landing strip for microlights.

Beaufort cow grazing the lush grass in the alpage above Refuge du Doran

5. Run on downwards, and at the first path junction turn L. You soon reach the track; follow it as it winds downwards and across the Plaine Joux plateau, past the buildings at **Les Trépas** and **Gadon**. The track contours L around the hillside here. When you reach the track junction at 1150m, ignore the turning uphill (which leads back to the Doran hut) and turn R then almost immediately L onto a small path signposted to Plan Chevalier.

6. Run past a small reservoir lake and keep following the trail downhill. Soon after crossing an ephemeral stream at 920m you reach a path junction at 880m where you fork R. This brings you out to the road very close to the car park where you started. (From the car park, runners who started from Sallanches should take Route d'Outrediere and retrace their outward steps back into the town.)

Getting the best from your bladder

When carrying a water bladder, squeeze all the air out of the bladder as you seal it. This will stop it sloshing around and moving on your back. Not only is the noise irritating, but bag movement could also cause painful sores on a longer run.

Route 22
Mont Truc

Start/Finish	Tourist office, Les Contamines (1167m/3828ft)
Distance	12.8km (8 miles)
Ascent/Descent	805m (2640ft)
Grade	Trail running, Level 1 (with 1km of fell running, Level 2)
Time	2hr 30min
High point	Mont Truc (1811m/5941ft)
Maps	IGN 3531 St Gervais 1:25,000, Rando Editions A1 Pays du Mont Blanc 1:50,000
Public transport	Train to Le Fayet, then bus to Les Contamines
Season	May to November

This short run is a good option if you have a few hours to spare, or half a day at most. It boasts stunning views of the Aiguille de Bionnassay and the Dômes du Miage, as well as taking in the summit of Mont Truc. Above the Chalets du Truc you're on open ground with indistinct tracks, so it's more akin to fell running. The objective is obvious, and you can choose the best line that suits you in terms of gradient.

> ### Safety
> This region is objectively safe when there's no snow cover, so there's a long running season in which to enjoy this route. Just ensure that there's no remaining snow on the descent from Truc to Miage.

1 Take the Route de la Frasse opposite the tourist office, which snakes its way up to a car park at the trailhead. Run up the hill and you'll find a cut-through between all the corners of the road, taking a straight line to **La Frasse**. When you arrive there, continue upwards onto the forest track past Les Granges de la Frasse.

2 Run through a wide gully, curving around to the L, and soon after turning R around the spur of the ridge, look out for a sign on the R for Chalets de Truc.

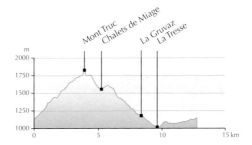

Leave the forestry track here and run a great section of single track through the woods, taking care as you run over the tree routes. Emerge onto another forestry trail and turn R uphill to reach a corner that doubles back on itself.

Follow the rising traverse until you emerge above the treeline into an open alpage. In front of you are the **Chalets du Truc**, and beyond them is the dome shape of Mont Truc. Run up **Mont Truc**, choosing your preferred line, and descend to the SSE towards the closest building. Just beyond it is a trail; turn L and descend steeply into the trees, emerging close to a bridge with the **Chalets de Miage** on the far side.

3 Turn L along the larger track before the bridge and run down the L bank of the river. Follow it, traversing downwards around Mont Truc, to a path junction at 1380m on its westerly aspect. Turn R and keep descending through

Running down to Chalets de Truc

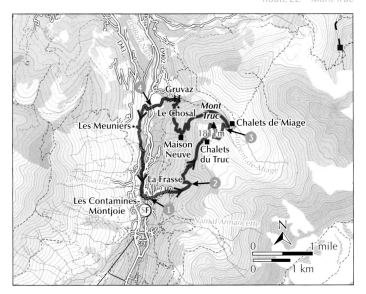

the farmyard at **Maison Neuve** and onwards to **Le Chosal**. Continue until you see the **Gruvaz** bridge and car park down to your R. Before the bridge, turn off L along a signposted trail towards Tresse and Le Ouy.

4 Take care on the road crossing, and once you've crossed the river, follow the road up R and then L, where it gives way to a trail. Follow the Tour du Mont Blanc signs towards Les Contamines. First you run through **Les Meuniers**, where you regain the road. Follow it across the river and turn R on the far bank; the river trail leads into **Les Contamines**, with a steep finish to emerge just behind the tourist office where you started.

Braking technique

When running off tracks, try not to brake by landing with your heels, as this makes you more prone to twisting an ankle or slipping. Try to run smoothly, letting gravity carry you down the hill.

Route 23
Mont Joly

Start/Finish	Tourist office, Les Contamines (1167m/3828ft)
Distance	19.4km (12 miles)
Ascent/Descent	1405m (4690ft)
Grade	Trail running, Level 3
Time	4hr 30min
High point	Mont Joly (2525m/8284ft)
Maps	IGN 3531 Megève/Col des Aravis 1:25,000, Rando Editions A1 Pays du Mont Blanc 1:50,000
Public transport	Train to Le Fayet, then bus to Les Contamines
Season	Late June to October

Running the exposed grassy ridgeline of Mont Joly is exhilarating, and traversing the mountain, with Mont Blanc to your right and the Rochers des Fiz ahead, is a visual feast. From the Chamonix valley, the summit of Mont Joly is often seen poking its pyramidal head over the skyline behind Prarion and Les Houches, begging to be run. The geology on Mont Joly differs from that around Chamonix, with the steep east-facing mountainside scored by ravines and outcrops, but the ridge crest is smooth and a delight to run.

① With your back to the tourist office, turn R and run along the high street until you start to leave the town. At a junction where the road continues to Le Lay, turn R and cross the bridge over the river. Follow the road up one switchback, passing the Club Alpin Français chalet on the R. Run ahead and cross the bridge over the Nant Fandraz before turning R up the road to **Le Baptieu**. As you enter the village, turn R at the junction and follow the road uphill.

② At the next sharp RH corner, the trail cuts off L to continue straight upwards and bypass several corners of the road before rejoining it at a bridge over the Roget stream. Follow the road upwards again, through two hairpins and to the hamlet of **Colombaz**. Take a track on the R, leave the road behind and start ascending. This is a wonderfully traditional farming area, and you pass the alpage buildings at Les Combettes and **La Tapée**. Just above the last buildings, at a height of 1680m, turn L onto a smaller path.

3 This leads you up and across the valley of the Ty stream and to a path junction at **La Borgia** (1873m). Turn L and run along a great trail that gradually ascends across the hillside, first through a bowl to the ruins at **La Tierce** (1972m). Here, above you are 13 streams feeding into the gully below. Run

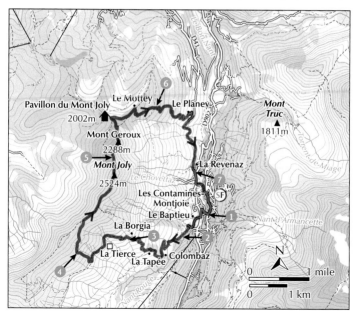

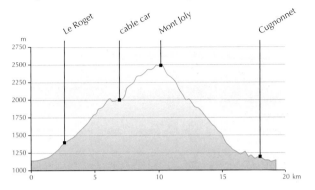

onwards across several more streams until you reach the Veleray ski lift. Just beyond it turn R onto a small track that zig-zags upwards below the cables.

4　Follow this track up to a path junction, where you turn R, then at the next junction ignore the L turn (which would take you back under the cables) and run SA. This path brings you to the ridge crest at 2354m, and all the hard work of the main ascent is soon forgotten as the view stretches for kilometres ahead while you traverse the ridgeline.

　　Run over the first summit, the Tête de la Combaz (2445m), after which there's a slight descent before climbing gently to **Mont Joly** at 2524m. There are stunning views at the summit cairn, as well as an orientation table to help you identify the surrounding peaks.

5　Continue running ahead and descend the spur over **Mont Geroux** (2288m), below which there's a steep descent to the **Pavillon du Mont Joly**, where you can get refreshments. Turn R here and follow the Tour du Pays du Mont Blanc to **Le Mottey**, then follow the track down R to Palengeard, where you leave the big track and cut SA down into the forest.

6　Run steeply downhill in the woods, under the power lines and past the buildings at Les Tuiles, to reach the road head at **Le Planey**. Follow the road down and keep R at a junction to run through Le Carteyron. The road gives way to a trail again, which crosses the stream valley ahead. At the buildings at Les Granges, keep on the RH path, ignoring the track dropping down to the L. Run along the descending traverse to arrive at the village of **La Revenaz**.

The ridge crest of Mont Joly in autumn

7 Reach a road, and turn R at a junction to cross the Cugnonnet stream bridge. Run along the road and cross the Chovettaz river bridge after the chapel, and immediately afterwards turn L down a track to cross the main river. On the far side of this bridge turn R to follow a section of the Tour du Mont Blanc and signs for the centre of **Les Contamines**. Make your way back to the start point at the tourist office.

Mental milestones

Where you have a significant height gain, such as on this run, it helps to identify points on the ascent that give you mental goals. For example, on this route at La Borgia you've done just over half the vertical ascent. Keeping these mental milestones helps to stop your brain playing tricks on you and wards off negative thoughts. For many runners it's the brain that gives up in a race well before the body, so to have a coping mechanism is an essential technique.

Route 24
Refuge de Tré-la-Tête

Start/Finish	Car park, Le Cugnon (1200m/3937ft)
Distance	13.7km (8½ miles)
Ascent/Descent	1005m (3300ft)
Grade	Trail running, Level 3
Time	3hr 15min
High point	Tré la Tête (1970m/6463ft)
Maps	IGN 3531 St Gervais 1:25,000, Rando Editions A1 Pays du Mont Blanc 1:50,000
Public transport	Train to Le Fayet, then bus to Le Cugnon via Les Contamines
Season	Mid June to September

The trails in this area yield some of the best running in the Contamines valley, and you really escape the crowds of the Tour du Mont Blanc. From the Tré la Tête mountain hut you share a section of route that climbers use to access the Conscrits hut for an ascent of the Dômes du Miage.

Safety

The Tré la Tête hut is only open during the suggested running season for this route, so you're guaranteed access to refreshments if you stick to that window. Huts are a great source of information, so if you're unsure of the conditions, call the hut you intend to run past on a route and get an update.

---

1 Set off up the trail from the toilet building in the car park, and almost immediately branch off on a LH trail ascending steeply up a stream gully with several zig-zags. Ignore two turnoffs to the R, even though they both lead to the Tré la Tête, and ascend past the buildings at **Les Feugiers**. Continue to a path junction at 1550m, where you join a section of the Tour du Pays du Mont Blanc.

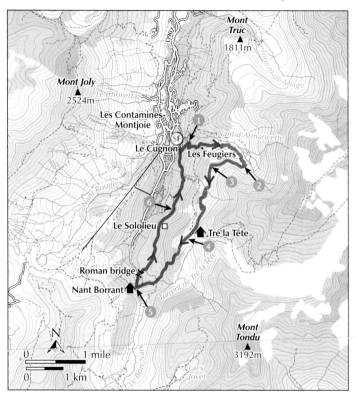

2 Work your way up and out of the treeline, into the Combe d'Armancette. A seemingly never-ending series of bends leads upwards to 1900m. Just when it seems you can't get any further without climbing, the path turns sharply R below the cliffs. Contour around this N aspect of the mountain in a slightly descending traverse.

3 Pass the small peak of Mont Freuge before turning S, and at a path junction at 1770m keep L to ascend again, now on the Chemin Claudius Bernard. At the next path split go R, and this trail leads you to the **Tré la Tête** mountain

The Tré-le-Tête refuge, with Mont Joly beyond

hut, whose terrace is a great place to take a rest and enjoy the views before starting your descent.

4 Beyond the hut, the trail to Nant Borrant drops in a SW direction. It's a steep slope, and you soon drop below the treeline. There are no path junctions to worry about, so you can focus on your running. At the bottom of the descent you arrive at the Cascade de Combe Noire waterfall; cross the

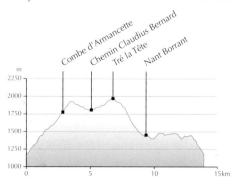

stream here and continue onwards towards Nant Borrant, passing a series of small farm buildings and crossing another bridge to reach the Tour du Mont Blanc track.

⑤ Turn R and run past **Nant Borrant**, continuing down the trail to a **Roman bridge** at 1392m where the river thunders below you in a deep gorge. On the far side of the bridge turn R and leave the TMB track behind you. The trail gently ascends through the area of La Rosière and onwards through alpage clearings past the ruins at **Le Sololieu** at 1480m, where you begin a descending traverse of a steep hillside.

⑥ After three stream crossings in quick succession – the last being the Nant des Grassenières – veer R at a path junction and ignore the path dropping down steeply to your L. Run along a great section of single track through the forest, crossing several more streams, until the path turns slightly uphill and you join another trail. Turn L and follow this across another stream, after which a path joins down from the R. Keep running ahead, and after a final stream crossing and four sharp corners you arrive back at the car park of Le Cugnon.

Shade or sun?

As this route is west-facing, it's cooler to run in the morning when you're in the shade. In the afternoon it becomes very warm, as the sun has moved around, so it's humid in the forest and there's little shade above the treeline.

Route 25
Tête Nord des Fours

Start/Finish	Gîte de la Nova, Les Chapieux (1549m/5082ft)
Distance	16.1km (10 miles)
Ascent/Descent	1175m (3855ft)
Grade	Trail running, Level 3 (with 4km of Level 4)
Time	4hrs
High point	Tête Nord des Fours (2756m/9042ft)
Maps	IGN 3531 St Gervais 1:25,000, Rando Editions A1 Pays du Mont Blanc 1:50,000
Public transport	Bus from Bourg St Maurice
Season	Mid July to September

This run explores some of the finest landscapes in the Beaufortain valley, taking in the magnificent viewpoint of the Tête Nord des Fours, looking upwards to Mont Blanc. This region is harder to access from Chamonix, but you can drive from Courmayeur over the Petil St Bernard pass to Bourg St Maurice and up to Les Chapieux. This is a very special region of the Alps, where farming traditions are strongly upheld, and the landscape is unspoiled and undeveloped. If you want to escape the tourist hotspots, this is a great choice.

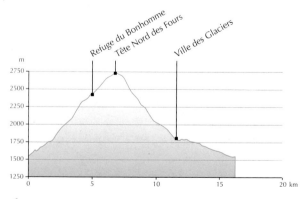

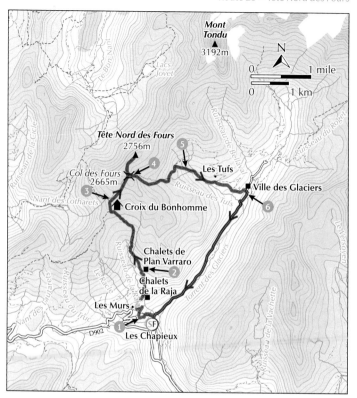

Safety

The late start of the recommended season for running this route is to allow any lingering snow patches on the Col des Fours to melt sufficiently so that runners can pass easily, without danger of sliding. If your navigation skills aren't too hot it's worth avoiding this area in poor weather, as the upper paths are very indistinct and the top has a big drop-off down towards the upper Contamines valley.

1 Starting opposite the Gîte de la Nova, the route follows the well-marked Tour du Mont Blanc trail in a N direction up the hillside, to the L of the electricity pylons. Follow the zig-zags up to the track at **Les Murs**, then turn R and follow the track across the bridge at **Chalets de la Raja** (1796m), where you veer L on the single track up the mountain, keeping the Raja river stream on your L.

2 Continue to ascend the hillside, crossing a series of streams and rocky outcrops as you gain altitude – the occasional hand may be required for stability. There's a brief respite in the gradient around the **Chalets de Plan Varraro** at 2013m before the trail steepens again to just above 2300m, where it turns L away from the pylons towards the **Refuge de la Croix du Bonhomme**.

This hut is spectacularly situated, with views across the Beaufortain region, and you can obtain refreshments here before your final ascent – but don't be tempted by the Leffe beer they have on tap!

3 Run straight up the path behind the hut, signposted for the TMB, to a path junction at 2479m where you turn R towards the Col des Fours.

Refuge de la Croix du Bonhomme

Looking back up to Col des Fours

Climb initially up a spur to the R of the stream before cutting beneath the pylons and entering the valley beneath the Tête Sud des Fours. The terrain becomes increasingly rocky, and the dark shales give way to a limestone cap. The route is marked with red blobs of paint on the rocks.

4　When you arrive at the **Col des Fours** (2665m), head N over the rock to reach the ridgeline, then turn slightly R and head in a NE direction to follow the ridge to the summit of the **Tête Nord des Fours**. Take in the views here before returning to the Col des Fours by the same route.

Descend from the pass by aiming down the fall line of the slope in a roughly SE direction. The ground is loose and often quite wet underfoot, but it's very runnable. Descend for 200m, at which point the path becomes more distinct and then turns L to cross a stream below a waterfall. There follows a series of stream crossings, and when you reach the 2200m contour you enter the Tufs valley and turn down the trail that drops into the valley floor.

5　Run alongside the stream to the far end of the valley, where you arrive at the buildings of **Les Tufs** (1993m). The trail keeps R of a farm track to cut between corners, bringing you out at the farm buildings of **Ville des**

Snow patches down from Col des Fours

Running on loose shale

There's a lot of loose shale on this route. To help keep stones out of your shoes, you could wear longer running socks and fold them down so they overlap the top of your shoes and act as a temporary fabric gaiter. You could also use calf compression guards to the same effect.

Glaciers. Here you can buy Beaufortain cheese, and there's a toilet block in the car park with taps to replenish your water bottles.

6 For the final section of the run, turn R and follow the road down the valley to **Les Chapieux** and you start point at Gîte de la Nova.

The Hospice du Grand St Bernard after snow (Route 31)

SWITZERLAND

Route 26
Mont de l'Arpille

Start	Trient church (1290m/4232ft)
Finish	SNCF station, Martigny (474m/1555ft)
Distance	15.5km (9¾ miles)
Ascent	770m (2525ft)
Descent	1610m (5280ft)
Grade	Trail running, Level 2
Time	3hr 15min
High point	Mont de l'Arpille (2085m/6840ft)
Maps	Swiss Topos 1324 Barbarine & 1325 Sembrancher 1:25,000, Swiss Topo 5003 Mont Blanc-Grand Combin 1:50,000
Public transport	Bus to Trient, and train from Martigny
Season	May to October

From the summit of Mont de l'Arpille you get one of the best views down the Rhone valley, all the way across to the Grand Combin, ahead to the Oberland, and back to Mont Blanc. For a relatively lowly summit the views are stupendous, and this is a great choice of route for someone visiting the area for the first time as it helps get your bearings. The trails are good underfoot, but note the proportion of ascent to descent for this run, as it's a long way all the way down into Martigny.

Safety

There are a few road crossings on this route, so take extra care.

---

① Starting from the distinctive bright pink church in the centre of Trient, follow the main road uphill and S out of the village. Almost immediately on the L is a sign marking a path that leads upwards to the Col de Forclaz. Run up this trail, and at the first junction turn L before crossing the road

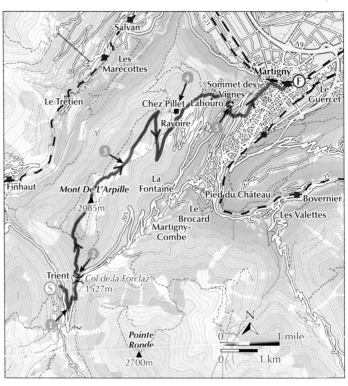

and soon reaching another junction with a flat trail. Turn L and quickly reach the **Col de Forclaz**.

2 Turn R and cross the pass, and you'll find a path on the L behind the hotel, signposted to Mont de l'Arpille. At the first path junction head L and ascend a series of bends up the steep hillside. Keep ascending in a N direction, and when you breach the treeline the summit of **Mont de l'Arpille** is just ahead, marked with a viewing table and signpost. Run SA past some avalanche fences and down to the obvious farm buildings at the l'Arpille alpage at 1800m.

Alpage de l'Arpille farm buildings

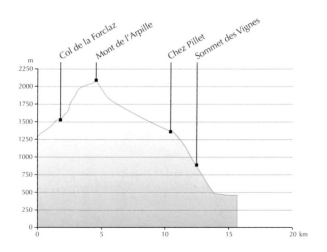

3 Look for a 4x4 track leading out of the alpage. Run along this and past a small parking area at the end of the alpage, from where you follow the track into forest. Continue to descend on this major path in large zig-zags, initially turning R, then L, to reach the road head. Follow the single road along past the car park to the corner at 1328m. Leave the road here and run straight on to the village of **Chez Pillet**.

4 At a junction veer R and run downhill through the village of Chez les Proz to Le Faylet. Cross R at the road and drop down on the trail to **Labouro**. The route to Martigny is well marked, and you arrive at the **Sommet des Vignes**, where you run through the vineyards on the last section of the route.

5 At a path junction just before the main road, take the RH trail that drops steeply down, re-crossing the road at 592m, to reach the old city gates at the Pont de Rossettan. Cross the Dranse river and turn L to run along it until just before the point at which a railway bridge crosses ahead of you. Turn R into town to return to **Martigny station**.

Preserving the knees

This route involves a descent of over 1600m, so it's one to avoid if you have problems with your knees – although you could consider running it in reverse from Martigny to Trient, to maximise ascent and minimise descent.

Route 27
Croix de Fer

Start/Finish	Trient church (1290m/4232ft)
Distance	16.6km (10¼ miles)
Ascent/Descent	1135m (3725ft)
Grade	Trail running, Level 3 (with 2km of Skyrunning, Level 3)
Time	4hrs
High point	Croix de Fer (2343m/7687ft)
Maps	IGN 3630 Chamonix 1:25,000, Rando Editions A1 Pays du Mont Blanc 1:50,000
Public transport	Bus to Trient from Vallorcine or Châtelard
Season	June to September

This circuit features amazing views of the Trient glacier, and takes you through rough and remote terrain on some of the least used trails in the Mont Blanc massif. You feel like you're running in the wilderness here. The route takes in the Col de Balme on the border with France, and the airy summit of the Croix de Fer, before running a section of UTMB down from Les Tseppes to Trient.

Safety

There are a few sections where you'll need to use your hands, so running poles might get in your way on this route. Don't be tempted to take in the summit of Croix de Fer if it's wet or stormy, or if there's any remnant snow, as it's very exposed. Instead, traverse across and down from the Col d'Arolette at 2277m to the Catogne path at 2065m, bypassing the summit.

---

1 From the pink church in Trient, follow Route 26 up to the flat trail near the Col de Forclaz. When you reach this, turn R and head S along the Bisse de Trient-Combe path. This small stream was once used to float blocks of ice down from the glacier to the road, from where carts took them into the villages.

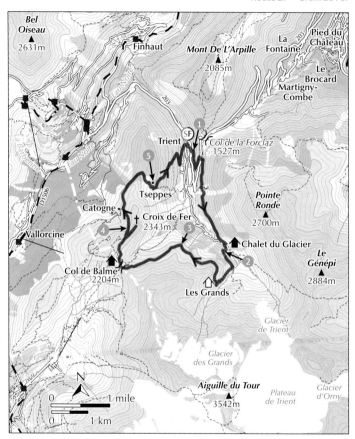

The Bisse is a wide trail with a very gradual upward gradient all the way to the **Chalet du Glacier** at 1583m, where you can get refreshments and a great view of the Trient Glacier above you.

2 Retrace your steps to the bridge below the chalet. Cross it, and on the far side turn L to ascend the path towards Les Grands. This climbs steeply, and above the small hut building at **Les Grands** (2113m) you ascend a steep stone ramp around a cliff as you traverse around the peak called Tronc du

View to Trient glacier from Les Grands

Berger. Follow the trail, on a slightly descending angle, to Le Remointse and a path junction at 2064m, taking care as you cross a few rock steps.

3 At the junction, turn L uphill and run the long traverse to **Col de Balme** (2204m). You can get refreshments at the hut, and take in the view along the Chamonix valley and up to Mont Blanc. Turn R and take a trail leading N then NW to the pass between Arolette and Croix de Fer. Turn R at the pass and follow the increasingly airy path to the **cross** marking the summit, and then follow the same route back to the pass before turning R.

First aid kit

There's a lot of rough ground on this trail, so abrasions and cuts from rocks are possible. Always carry a very basic running first aid kit to treat these, including a dressing, strapping tape and an antiseptic wipe.

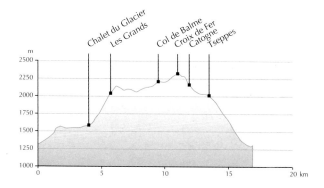

④ Take the LH trail at the junction just beyond the pass and run down to the Catogne path at 2065m. Turn R, then L at the next junction and run down the path to Pas des Moutons (1996m), where you round the shoulder of the mountain and the Trient valley comes into view again.

⑤ Run down past the buildings at **Tseppes**, and into the treeline, to reach a path junction at 1760m. Turn L here and follow the path down past the spot heights on the corners at 1540m and 1417m. At the next path junction you meet a major forest track, above Le Praillon. Turn L down this and run into **Trient**, crossing the bridge behind the church where you started.

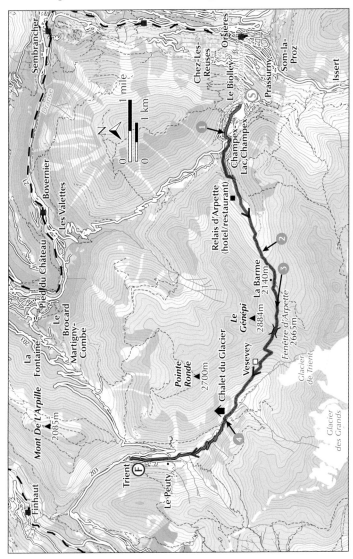

Route 28
Fenêtre d'Arpette

Start	SE end of Lac de Champex (1468m/4816ft)
Finish	Trient village (1290m/4232ft)
Distance	14.4km (9 miles)
Ascent	1145m (3755ft)
Descent	1320m (4330ft)
Grade	Trail running, Level 3 (with 2km of Level 4)
Time	4hrs
High point	Fenêtre d'Arpette (2665m/8743ft)
Maps	IGN 3630 OT Chamonix 1:25,000, Rando Editions A1 Pays du Mont Blanc 1:50,000
Public transport	Bus to Champex, and from Trient
Season	July to September
Note	Check the weather forecast for mention of diurnal instability, afternoon storms or convection cells, as any of these might indicate a likelihood of electric storms in the afternoon. Even if the forecast is looking stable, you're advised to set off early.

The high point of this run provides a great view of the Trient glacier, and is also the joint highest pass on any of the variations of the Tour du Mont Blanc (TMB). The upper section is tough, but you're rewarded with superb views of the glacier throughout the descent.

Safety

There is steep ground on either side of the Fenêtre d'Arpette, and if there's any significant snow cover at all, crampons and ice axe are required. Runners should only undertake the route when all the snow on steeper ground has melted, as a slip on this terrain would have serious consequences. Note that there are often remnant snow patches on this route throughout the year. If in doubt, follow the Bovine trail (see Route 37, Stage 3) from Champex to Trient.

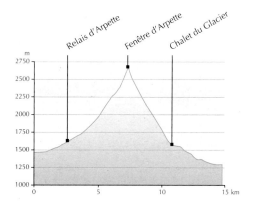

1. Start running NW along the road past the lake in Champex, and head up the hill towards the Breya ski lift. As the road turns sharply L, there's a track on the L signposted to the Val d'Arpette. Run along this, and next to a small lake turn R on the TMB path to pass beneath the Breya lift cables.

   The path follows a *bisse* – a small irrigation stream. Contour around the hillside, following the bisse, and when you reach the road turn R up the valley to the **Relais d'Arpette**, where you can get refreshments.

2. Continue running up the track, which gets rougher and narrower as you ascend into the upper valley. Keep an eye out for signposts to the Fenêtre d'Arpette. The path weaves across the base of the valley, crossing the stream. As you reach the 2100m contour at **La Barme**, the valley ahead narrows. As the trail steepens just beyond this outcrop, turn R at a path junction. As you ascend, the Fenêtre d'Arpette is obvious as the lowest point on the broken skyline ahead.

   Above 2250m the terrain becomes wilder and more remote, and the path becomes increasingly rough as you ascend over loose stones and boulders. There are many small cairns to show you the way to the base of the final steep climb. Take your time on this section, as there's a lot of loose rock, and remember Edward Whymper's advice to do nothing in haste, and to look well to each step. Walk in some sections if necessary.

3. The final slope is a slog, but at **Fenêtre d'Arpette** you're rewarded with stunning views of the Trient glacier, which has been hidden from view until now.

Anyone who studied geography at school will have no problems identifying the lateral and terminal moraines of the glacier, and the smooth slabs revealed by the all-too-obvious glacial retreat.

After a quick break, follow the path down and to the R into the Trient valley. It's a steep descent, over rough ground initially, before you reach a good path that zig-zags down past the ruined buildings at **Vesevey** (2096m). Keep running down into the treeline, and soon reach the **Chalet du Glacier** (1583m), where refreshments are available.

Running on the Bisse de Trient

4 Just below the buvette is a footbridge. Run across this, turn immediately R and continue for a short while until you reach a small road. Head L and run down to **Le Peuty** and on towards Trient. In the steeper upper section you'll find a series of cut-throughs, where tracks shorten the corners of the road. Run over the stream of the Nant Noir, and soon arrive in **Trient** village.

Crossing bouldery ground

This route traverses several boulder fields, so it's worth wearing something to cover your legs and protect from abrasions while running, or in case of a fall. Leggings or long socks are ideal. These will also keep you warm when the cool katabatic winds blow down from the Trient glacier.

Route 29
Cabane d'Orny

Start	SE end of Lac de Champex (1468m/4816ft)
Finish	Bus stop, Praz de Fort (1151m/3776ft)
Distance	15.6km (9¾ miles)
Ascent	1325m (4345ft)
Descent	1645m (5400ft)
Grade	Trail running, Level 3
Time	4hr 15min
High point	Cabane d'Orny (2826m/9271ft)
Maps	IGN 3630 OT Chamonix 1:25,000 or Swiss Topo 1345 Orsières 1:25,000, Swiss Topo 5003 Mont Blanc-Grand Combin 1:50,000
Public transport	Bus to Champex, and from Praz de Fort
Season	July to September

This run will appeal to those who love wild landscapes. The highlight is the view from the Cabane d'Orny, which is perched on rocks above a lake at the foot of the Orny Glacier – a tongue of the main Trient Glacier. The route also takes you to the beautiful Saleina valley, and finishes at the picture-postcard village of Praz de Fort, where the traditional wooden houses are perched on granite blocks capped with rat stones to keep mice and rats out of the grain that was once stored there.

1 Run NW up the road away from the lake in Champex, towards the Breya cable car, and where the road curves L, exit L onto a track towards the Val d'Arpette. Ignore the TMB track turnoff and keep the small lake to your R. Continue up the track, and at the junction beneath the cables of the Breya ski lift, turn R and continue around the hillside and across the ski piste to a path junction at 1592m.

There are two L turns alongside each other: take the second one, which ascends a spur in the trees. At a path junction, keep L and continue upwards into a gully. A series of corners climbs the hillside of the ski area, and you pass below another lift at 2000m. Soon after, at the next junction, turn L and

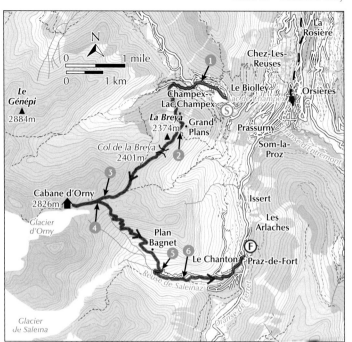

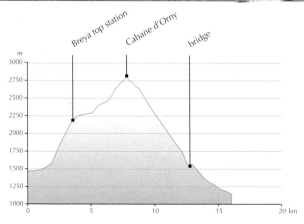

Cabane d'Orny and its glacial lake

> ### Safety
>
> The upper section of this route goes through periglacial landscapes, where you're often running on recently uncovered moraines that can be loose underfoot. Moraines become less stable in wet weather, so this route is best saved for a dry day.

continue to **Grand Plans** (2194m) – the top station of the Breya lift. Follow the path in a SW direction to a cross, following signposts for Cabane d'Orny.

2 Run past the cross, ignoring a path dropping down to the L, and soon after ignore a path cutting up R to the summit of **La Breya**. Your path traverses the hillside just to the L of the ridgeline, and you pass below the **Col de la Breya**. Ahead the path looks blocked by the cliffs, but it contours up and across to the L into the upper valley. As you near the stream, another path joins in from the L. Continue upwards on increasingly rough moraines.

3 The path braids slightly, but all options lead in the same direction. Make a mental note of the location of a path junction at 2691m, close to a cross

> ### Running on moraine
>
> When running on moraines you'll find poles useful for balance, but ensure that they have a very small snow basket (or none at all) on their base, as it's easy for the poles to become trapped under moraine and create a trip hazard. Don't run with your hands in the pole wrist loops, so you can drop a pole if it becomes snagged.

below the Lac d'Orny, as you'll return to this point later. Continue upwards, and the mountain hut comes into view, perched on top of a rocky outcrop to the R of a small glacial lake. Run up to the **Cabane d'Orny** – the high point of your run – where you can stop to rest and get refreshments.

4. Run back down to the lower lake and the path junction at 2691m, and turn R on a path that initially heads due E and then turns in a progressively S direction, to cut R of the Pointes des Chevrettes cliffs. The path zig-zags below these peaks, descending steeply into the upper Saleina valley. It stays on the true L bank of the Orny stream, and all the main corners are marked with spot heights on the Swiss maps.

5. As you approach the treeline, turn R at three successive path junctions – the first at **Plan Bagnet** (1777m) and then finally at the road by the buildings at 1540m. Follow the road uphill for a short while before cutting L on a track to cross the stream at 1560m. On the far side, follow the track up to a L turn. Take this, and run along a fantastic trail on the R bank of the stream.

6. Keep on running all the way down to a bridge at 1354m, where you turn L across the river, then turn R at a path junction before the road. This trail descends alongside the road, and then rejoins it at 1220m. Follow the road downhill to the T-junction, where you turn L.

Run across the bridge at **Le Chanton**, and soon after take a little track on the R, which leads through the oldest part of the village of **Praz de Fort** to arrive at the main road next to a bridge over the main river. This is the end of the run, and the bus stop here is for buses descending the valley to Orsières.

Route 30
Mont Fourchon

Start/Finish	Hospice du Grand Saint Bernard (2469m/8100ft)
Distance	7km (4¼ miles)
Ascent/Descent	605m (1985ft)
Grade	Trail running, Level 4
Time	2hrs
High point	Mont Fourchon (2902m/9521ft)
Maps	Swiss Topo 1365 Grand Saint Bernard 1:25,000, Swiss Topo 5003 Mont Blanc-Grand Combin 1:50,000
Public transport	Bus to Grand Saint Bernard
Season	July to September

This run can be done in its own right, or as an extension to Route 31 for those staying overnight at the Hospice du Grand Saint Bernard. The summit of Mont Fourchon offers excellent views of the whole Mont Blanc massif.

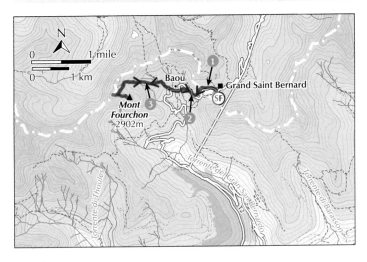

Safety

Apart from the first and last kilometre, this run is entirely in Italy, where the number for mountain rescue is 118. This differs from the usual 112 across most of Europe, as the Aosta valley is an autonomous region of Italy.

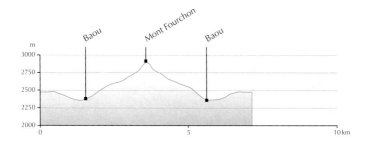

1. From the front door of the Hospice du Grand Saint Bernard, turn L. A path contours around the lake above the road and brings you to the statue of Saint Bernard. It's a striking sight, with the jagged tooth of the Pain de Sucre (2900m) behind, and you can just see the summit of Mont Fourchon (2902m) to its R. From here it looks inaccessible, but there's an easy route up the bowl to the R of the peak.

2. Just beyond the statue, take the path that drops down and crosses the road, to the L of a huge avalanche tunnel. The path then swings R and curves around the hillside down to buildings at 2352m, where you turn R and cross the road once again to ascend above the buildings at **Baou**. Cross a stream and ascend the L side of the gully to reach another path junction at 2500m. Keep L here and ignore the path off R, which ascends to the Fenêtre de Ferret.

3. Continue running along the path, passing a small lake on your R. Above 2600m the terrain becomes rougher underfoot, and the path is less distinct. Keep working your way up this wide bowl of the hillside, following the same W direction until you reach 2780m, when the path veers L to traverse almost due S and reach a small col. Be wary when approaching this, as there's a big

167

The Saint Bernard of Menthon statue

drop-off on the far side. Turn R and run the final steps to reach the top of **Mont Fourchon**.

The views from the summit make the effort worthwhile, with a complete panorama in every direction. You can see the Hospice far below, looking very small from this vantage point, while ahead is the bulk of the Mont Blanc massif. Once you've taken in the view, the return route is the exact inverse of the ascent, and you follow your track all the way back to the **Hospice du Grand Saint Bernard**.

Exploding bladders and how to avoid them

Don't be tempted to pour fizzy soft drinks into a hydration bladder, as the combination of being shaken and the gas expanding at altitude is likely to cause an explosion. In addition, it's very difficult to clean the tubes and reservoir effectively after sugary drinks have been in them.

Route 31
Cols Fenêtre and Chevaux

Start	Village shop, La Fouly (1593m/5226ft)
Finish	Town centre, Bourg St Pierre (1632m/5354ft)
Distance	27.5km (17 miles)
Ascent	1780m (5840ft)
Descent	1765m (5790ft)
Grade	Trail running, Level 3 (with 7km of Level 4)
Time	7hrs
High point	Col des Chevaux (2714m/8904ft)
Maps	Swiss Topos 1345 Orsières and 1365 Grand Saint Bernard 1:25,000, Swiss Topo 5003 Mont Blanc-Grand Combin 1:50,000
Public transport	Train to Martigny, then bus to La Fouly and from Bourg St Pierre
Season	July to September
Note	You pass a border post on the road from Italy to the Hospice du Grand Saint Bernard, which is a few metres across the border into Switzerland. It's very unlikely you'll be stopped for a check, but don't forget your passport just in case.

This route starts and ends in Switzerland, and you dip into Italy between the two high passes, and also visit the Hospice du Grand Saint Bernard. The running is challenging, with technical terrain and two high cols to cross, as well as significant ascent and descent. The area is steeped in history, with the monastery established by Bernard of Menthon on the Col du Mont Joux in 1047, Napoleon crossing with his army in 1800, and of course the Saint Bernard dogs, which were originally bred by the monks.

1 From the village shop next to Auberge des Glaciers, start running up the valley out of La Fouly with the ski lifts up on your L. Ignore a road turning R across a bridge, and follow the small road cutting up the hillside on the L towards the farm at **Le Barfay** (1820m). Follow the switchbacks of the road, then at the farm keep R and run along the contour track in a SSE direction. This track braids and descends slightly, but always keep high, and it brings you to the uppermost buildings of **Ferret** village.

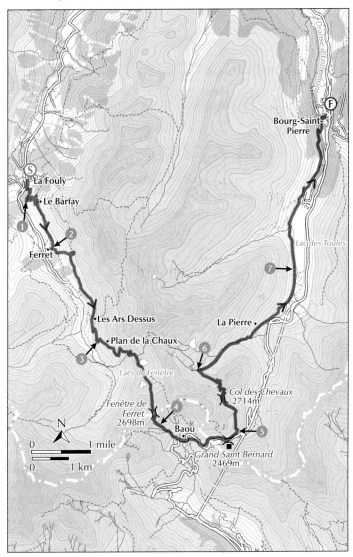

Safety

Ensure that your navigation skills are sufficient to cope in low visibility, as the trail is not always obvious. Don't rely on a GPS, as batteries can fail or the unit can easily be broken. As with all the runs in this book, carry a map and compass at all times.

2 Turn L and run up the trail towards the obvious ravine ahead. Ignore a RH turn near the 1800m contour, and run R into the mouth of the gully at 1898m. Here turn R and traverse around the mountain on a long section of great running towards the upper valley. At a path

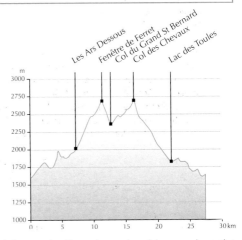

junction keep L, and after crossing three streams in quick succession arrive at **Les Ars Dessus** (1955m). Join the track just beyond, cross the stream, and take a cut-through on the L to rejoin the track up to **Plan de la Chaux** (2041m).

3 Here the track ends, and you turn L uphill towards the **Lacs de Fenêtre**. Twist and turn through a steeper gully just below the lakes before arriving at a path junction next to a cross at 2467m. Turn R and run past the first lake, then ignore a turnoff to the L and continue up the spur between the next two lakes. This trail leads towards the Fenêtre de Ferret (2698m) over increasingly rough ground. The pass is the Italian border, and the path drops steeply down on the far side.

4 Descend the zig-zags, and at a path junction continue downhill towards the buildings at **Baou**, close to the road. Keep on the track as it crosses the road, turn L at the path junction just below, and aim towards the Grand Saint Bernard pass. The path crosses the road again to the R of the avalanche

tunnel, and as you reach the ridge crest above, you see the statue of Saint Bernard with the devil in shackles at his feet. Keep on the path that traverses above the road around the lake ahead to arrive at the **Hospice du Grand Saint Bernard**.

Lunch at the Hospice du Grand Saint Bernard

5. Follow the road slightly downhill on the far side of the pass, and on the L you soon see a path cutting across the rocky ground. Run onwards to cross a rocky ridge at 2572m, then L and onwards to contour up and around the bowl to the **Col des Chevaux (2714m)** ahead. Adjust your speed for this section, as there's a lot of steep ground and loose rock. On the far side of the pass, the trail descends 300m on steep switchbacks to cross a gully. Take extra care on this descent as it's the most technical section of the route.

6. At a path junction at 2409m, turn R to run down the length of the Drone valley towards farm buildings at **La Pierre**, keeping L at another path junction just above the buildings at 2100m. Run along the slowly descending path in a NE direction, towards the lower valley floor and a footbridge at 1978m. Stay on the L bank of the river, and after passing the Saint Bernard tunnel entrance and Bourg Saint Bernard ski area, keep L again at a path junction. Keep running, and you'll see the reservoir of the **Lac des Toules** ahead of you.

7. Run the length of the lake, and just before the dam wall, the trail gives way to a road. Follow this past the dam and onward to a sharp R corner, where a trail cuts SA and down into the Dranse d'Entremont valley. It's signposted to Bourg Saint Pierre, but at a path junction at 1712m keep R and stay on this trail through the forests. At another path junction turn R to cross the bridge at 1591m and run the final section into the centre of **Bourg Saint Pierre**.

A night in a cell

In order to enjoy the area more, you could split this run into two sections by booking into the monastery for a night. The monks will welcome travellers every night of the year, even in the depths of winter. They offer a reasonably priced half-board stay, including an evening meal, a bed for the night, and breakfast the next morning. Tel +41 (0)277 871 236

The steep descent to the Col Sapin (Route 32)

ITALY

On the Mont de la Saxe ridge

Route 32
Mont de la Saxe

Start/Finish	Car park, Planpincieux (1564m/5131ft)
Distance	17km (10½ miles)
Ascent/Descent	1095m (3590ft)
Grade	Trail running, Level 3 (1km quite exposed)
Time	3hr 30min
High point	Tête de la Tronche (2584m/8477ft)
Maps	IGC 107 Monte Bianco Courmayeur 1:25,000, Rando Editions A1 Pays du Mont Blanc 1:50,000
Public transport	Bus to Courmayeur, then to Planpincieux
Season	June to October

This route comprises a superb ridgeline overlooking the vast south face of the Mont Blanc massif. It's one of the best viewpoints of Mont Blanc, and for the most part the ridge is broad and very runnable. There's a sting on the tail, however, with a more exposed section over Tête de la Tronche, and a steep descent to Col Sapin. The route involves a vertical kilometre of ascent, but due to the geology and elevation it's largely above the treeline, providing great views all day long.

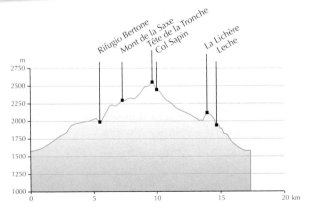

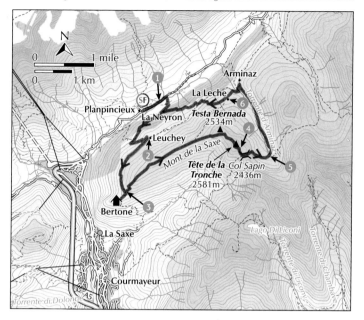

Safety

Avoid this route in rain, as the Tête de la Tronche is not a place to be in an electric storm. The route clears quickly of snow each year as most of it is exposed to the sun. A section of the Tour du Mont Blanc is followed and is much frequented by hikers, so information on conditions is readily available from the Rifugio Bertone, which is situated on the route (+39 0165 844 612).

1 From the car park at Planpincieux, follow the road up the valley for about a kilometre to a small chapel on the L and a bridge on the R. Cross the river here, and slanting up R across the hillside ahead of you is a jeep track. Run along this track, gaining height steadily, with views back down to the valley below. Pass some old farm buildings next to the track before taking a sharp L turn towards **Leuchey**. Signposts direct you from here towards the Rifugio Bertone.

2 Just above the hamlet of Leuchey, ignore the track off to the L and continue to Bertone. The trail enters a beautiful section of forest where the path is soft underfoot. Ascend at a gradual gradient to contour around the mountain and reach a viewpoint situated just above the **Rifugio Bertone**. If you're low on water it's worth dropping down to the hut to replenish your supplies, as there's no drinkable water ahead for the next hour or two.

3 Turn L up the hillside, following signs for Mont de la Saxe and Testa Bernarda. Initially the path is so steep as to be almost unrunnable, but after quarter of an hour it eases off as the ridgeline is reached. Ahead of you is at least an hour of the most spectacular running you'll encounter, as you follow the broad shoulder of the Saxe ridge. Towards the end of the ridge, skirt R across the slopes of **Testa Bernarda** to gain the summit ridge of **Tête de la Tronche**. Take care here, as the path is suddenly exposed and airy. Keep just to the R of the ridge crest.

4 After the summit, the track drops sharply towards the Col Sapin. There's a lot of broken rock and erosion on this part of the trail, so take your time and choose your route wisely. At the **Col Sapin** (2436m) the trail turns L to

Testa Bernada with Mont Blanc beyond

Traversing the Testa Bernada

descend into the Armina valley. In bad weather, an escape route from the col is to turn R and descend into Courmayeur through the village of La Saxe.

5   As you run from Col Sapin into the Armina valley you'll see some ruined farm buildings ahead, and a river running down the valley. There are paths down either side of the river, and it doesn't matter which one you take, although the track on the far side is more defined. Veer L down the valley until you reach its end.

6   If you descended the near side of the valley you'll reach La Lichère (2115m), and if you came down on the far side you'll arrive at **Arminaz** (2009m). From either point, take the trails descending L to reach **La Leche** (1902m). Below here the trail descends to reach **La Neyron** and the jeep track you ascended at the start of the run. Follow this back down to the bridge, and then along the road to **Planpincieux**.

Conserving water

In common with many trail runs in the mountains, there's no regular water supply on this route. To help conserve your water, focus on two things: reduce the amount you sweat by removing clothing before you get too hot; and try to breathe through your nose rather than your mouth in order to reduce moisture loss.

Route 33
Tête Entre Deux Sauts

Start	Bus stop, La Vachey (1642m/5387ft)
Finish	Bus stop, Pra Sec (1620m/5315ft)
Distance	11.4km (7 miles)
Ascent	1025m (3360ft)
Descent	1040m (3410ft)
Grade	Trail running, Level 3 (with 500m of Level 4)
Time	3hrs
High point	Tête Entre Deux Sauts (2729m/8953ft)
Maps	IGC 107 Monte Bianco Courmayeur 1:25,000, Rando Editions A1 Pays du Mont Blanc 1:50,000
Public transport	Bus to La Vachey, and from Pra Sec
Season	July to October
Note	In the summer months afternoon convection storms often bubble up in mountains, so ensure that you start early so as to be safely off the exposed ridgeline by mid-afternoon at the latest. If you're unsure on this route, consider truncating the circuit at the Pas Entre Deux Sauts.

Only a few trail running routes reach an actual summit, and the panorama from the Tête Entre Deux Sauts is one of the finest. On a clear day you can see the huge south faces of the entire Mont Blanc massif, from the Col de la Seigne on the Franco-Italian border, across to the Grandes Jorasses and then Mont Dolent on the Swiss-Italian border above the Grand Col Ferret. Just to make the day even more perfect, there's the option of stopping off at the luxurious Rifugio Bonatti for refreshments.

Safety

This route is north-facing, so it should not be undertaken too early in the season, allowing time for the snow patches to melt. Conversely, the summit ridge of the peak can often be dry as early as March, due to strong prevailing winds blowing the snow off, whereas the bowls below the Pas Entre Deux Sauts can keep snow well into June. You can call the team at Rifugio Bonatti (tel +39 0165 869 055) to get information about the current conditions.

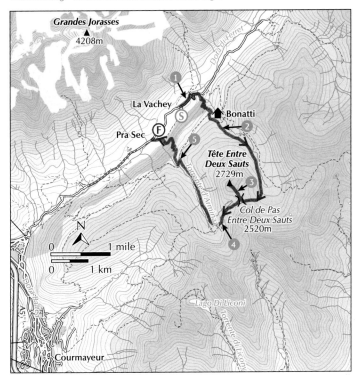

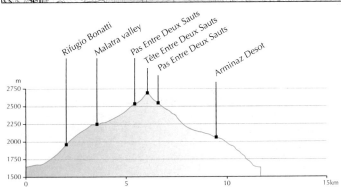

1 From the bus stop at La Vachey, follow the road up the valley for just over a kilometre until you see signposts to the Rifugio Bonatti on the R. The trail leads through a mature forest, steadily gaining height towards the treeline. The route is well signposted, and when you breach the treeline at 1800m you can soon see the **Rifugio Bonatti** just above you. Continue to the hut, where you can stop to refill your water bottles and get refreshments.

2 Behind the hut to the RH side, the trail leads up the Malatra valley. Pass a few abandoned farm buildings – many with their roofs collapsed from the weight of the winter snows. As you gain the upper valley the trail levels out and you can run at a steady pace. Just before the valley headwall, the path veers R and climbs to the **Pas Entre Deux Sauts** (2520m).

3 Ascend to the R and follow the increasingly sharp ridge. After the initial false summit above the pass, you soon see the long ridge leading to the main summit. The path is faint but the route is clear, and the **summit** is marked with a cairn from which you can see the Rifugio Bonatti far below.

Approaching the Rifugio Bonatti

Coping with slippery rock

This region is geologically complex, as it's on the edge of the granite of the main Mont Blanc massif and has a mixture of shale and limestone. These rocks provide a more rolling landscape but less grip underfoot than the friction of granite, so take shoes with good grips. Poles are ideal for this type of terrain – especially on the more exposed upper section of the summit ridge – to provide both traction and balance.

Descending the forests near Armina

4. Retrace your tracks to the pass and turn R down into the Armina valley. Descend steeply until you reach some old farm buildings, where there should be clean water in the stream to replenish your water bottles. Head down the Armina valley, crossing some boulder fields and rougher patches, to reach another farm at the foot of the valley at 2009m.

5. Keep the stream on your L and take the path descending steeply below the buildings. At the path crossroads at 1830m, take the L path down to the hamlet of **Pra Sec** in the valley, where you reach the road and a bus stop, or return along the valley floor trail described in Route 34.

Route 34
Italian Val Ferret

Start/Finish	Funivie Monte Bianco cable car station, Palud (1370m/4494ft)
Distance	12.5km (7¾ miles)
Ascent/Descent	305m (1000ft)
Grade	Trail running, Level 1
Time	2hrs
High point	La Vachey (1642m/5387ft)
Maps	IGC 107 Monte Bianco Courmayeur 1:25,000, Rando Editions A1 Pays du Mont Blanc 1:50,000
Public transport	Bus to Courmayeur, then Palud
Season	May to November

If you're looking for a shorter run, in stunning scenery, look no further than this route up the Italian Val Ferret. It's surrounded by some of the tallest peaks in the Alps, and the views up the south faces of the Grandes Jorasses and Mont Blanc are breathtaking. As a further incentive, the coffee and ice cream in Italy are simply wonderful, so take the time to treat yourself. In addition, as this is effectively an out-and-back run, due to the narrowness of the valley you can truncate it at any stage you wish. There's no need for running poles on this terrain, or heavier mountain waterproofs, so you can travel light and enjoy moving unencumbered.

Safety

Don't be tempted to lengthen this run by starting in Courmayeur, as in recent years there have been a lot of rockfalls and landslides from the western flank of Mont de la Saxe, affecting the footpath between Courmayeur and Palud. If you follow the road you'll be protected by the reinforced banks that have been built to contain any further landslips.

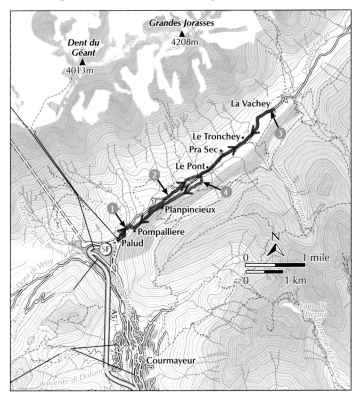

1 Start running up the road from the cable car station, past the car park on the R, and into the first couple of switchbacks. Run past a white barrier, which will be lowered across the road when it's closed due to avalanche risk in winter or when the car park is full. Continue up the road, keeping R where it splits for traffic ascending the valley. Cross a small road bridge, turn immediately R and descend the trail into the forest.

The path soon brings you to a narrow footbridge across the Doire de Ferret river. On its far side, veer L onto the main track. This leads upwards through the alpage to the buildings at **Pompalliere** before easing off as it follows the riverbank again. Ahead you'll see a bridge: cross this and turn

R onto a trail leading up to Planpincieux. The path ascends past some old buildings before reaching a driveway that leads to the road.

2 Turn R and follow the road to the car park at **Planpincieux** on your L. From this point onwards there's a wide selection of trails to your L running parallel to the road and ascending the valley. Many of these are used by the local horse riding school, and often follow sections of the winter cross-country trails, so they're well established. It doesn't matter which you follow, as they're all more pleasant than taking the small road that ascends the valley, and are always within a few hundred metres of it.

Run past the hamlets of **Le Pont**, with its avalanche-damaged buildings, then Le Tronchey, and onwards to **Pra Sec**. To the R of the river you'll see a golf course, which remains snow-covered for half the year. Just after **Le Tronchey**, most paths divert close to the road to avoid a marshy area of ground. Beyond the buildings at Pra Sec, a plain opens out on the valley floor, and a good trail leads straight across the open area.

View to the south face of Grandes Jorasses, taken from above Le Pont

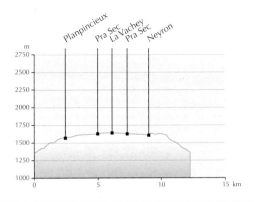

Chapel at Le Pont in the winter snow

Winter runs

In the winter months, when the valley's open and safe from avalanche risk, you can adapt this route to run along the road from Palud to Planpincieux, from which point the road is left snow-covered but is pisted as a walking track. It's possible to run along the route of the road to La Vachey and back, but don't be tempted to venture off to the sides, as the edges of this valley are frequently affected by avalanches.

3 At the far side of this, look out for a road bridge on the R, and cross it to arrive at **La Vachey**. As the name suggests, this was once the main dairy for the Italian Val Ferret. The green shuttered building at the far end of the hamlet is now an excellent café, famed for its thick hot chocolate, and the café walls are covered with hundreds of photos of the Grivel family who worked there. This family subsequently became famed for the manufacture of crampons and ice axes in nearby Courmayeur.

4 After stopping for refreshments, return along one of the valley trails to Le Pont. Join the road here, pass a small chapel on the R after a few hundred metres, and almost immediately on the L there's a bridge over the river at 1610m. Cross it, and on the far side follow a track up to the R. As you ascend beyond a small switchback, ignore a track off to the L and take the path off down to the R immediately afterwards.

This path drops slowly towards the river again, and then keeps to the true L bank and follows it down the valley. Run through two sections of woodland, and after the second, spot on your R the Pompalliere bridge that you crossed earlier. Ignore it, and retrace your initial route back past the buildings at Pompalliere, then across the footbridge down on your R to regain the road. Turn L and follow the road back to **Palud**.

Route 35
Col d'Arp

Start/Finish	Bus station, Courmayeur (1210m/3969ft)
Distance	21.6km (13½ miles)
Ascent/Descent	1715m (5625ft)
Grade	Trail running, Level 3
Time	5hr 15min
High point	Col d'Arp (2570m/8431ft)
Maps	IGC 107 Monte Bianco Courmayeur 1:25,000, Rando Editions A1 Pays du Mont Blanc 1:50,000
Public transport	Bus to Courmayeur
Season	July to September
Note	There are plenty of good water sources in the streams on this route, so 1L of water is enough to set off with.

This route follows the first section of the longest trail race in the world: the Tor des Géants – a 330km loop around the mountains on each side of the Aosta valley, involving 24,000m of vertical height gain. The race passes the four mountain ranges of Mont Blanc, Gran Paradiso, Monte Rosa and the Matterhorn, with a time barrier of 150 hours. Fear not: this route only does the first ascent, and you do a nice loop back to Courmayeur.

Safety

This area, and especially the ridge crest near to the Col d'Arp, can be a high lightning strike risk area in afternoon convection storms, so ensure that you start fairly early, to be over the pass before mid-afternoon at latest.

---

1 Set off from the main square and bus station in Courmayeur and run along the road to **Dolonne**, going through the underpass beneath the main road to Aosta. Run across the river bridge and follow the road as it curves up to the L on the far side. Continue until the road gives way to a trail; you'll now follow route number 1A on the signposts as far as Col d'Arp. Run upwards into the trees, and some alpage clearings, and between the buildings at **Champtoret**.

② Veer L into the bowl of the Vallon d'Arp and keep to the R of the stream. Follow the track up above the treeline to reach a trailhead at the hamlet of **Arp** (2138m). Keep running upwards, with the pass now obvious ahead. The altitude will slow you down slightly, so don't push too hard on this final climb. Watch out also for loose rocks on the path.

③ Finally the **Col d'Arp** (2570m) is reached, and you see the wild landscape of the Vallon de la Youlaz ahead of you. Look for the path turning off sharp L into the Youlaz valley and down to the buildings at the base of the slope. The route is signposted as number 4 now, and leads towards the main valley via La Balme and then La Thuile. Drop down this path and run past buildings at **Reggiani**, then continue all along the valley to the buildings at **Youlaz**.

④ Just after Youlaz, take a path on the L signposted for Tsa and Elevaz. Pass into the forest for a while and descend to **Tsa**, where you turn R to take the

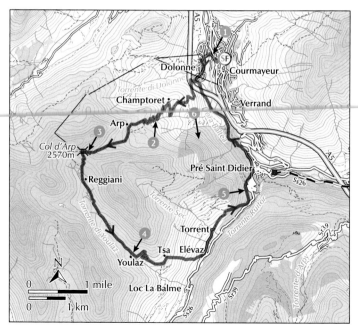

Italian or French?

Don't worry too much if you don't speak any Italian: most people in this region also speak fluent French, as it was part of the independent Savoie kingdom until just over 150 years ago.

path dropping down again to reach **Elevaz** (1302m). At the church in the village centre, bend L and follow the road to **Torrent**, where you follow the path on a slight rising traverse below Quiedro, and then turn R on path number 6 to descend to Pré Saint Didier.

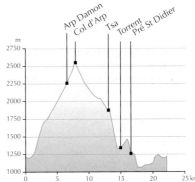

5 The path cuts through the corners of the road descending to **Pré Saint Didier**, which is laid out like loops of spaghetti up the hillside. As you approach town, stay on the road as it veers to the L, and then leave the road at the apex of the final R corner. Continue SA towards Courmayeur on route number 1.

6 Follow this well-marked track, which stays close to the river, until it passes below the motorway flyover. Just beyond, it cuts up the hillside to reach Dolonne; turn R on the road to retrace the initial section of the route into the centre of **Courmayeur**.

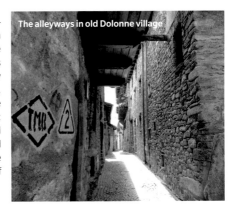

The alleyways in old Dolonne village

Route 36
Punta della Croce

Start/Finish	Arpy village (1682m/5518ft)
Distance	19.7km (12¼ miles)
Ascent/Descent	925m (3035ft)
Grade	Trail running, Level 2
Time	3hr 45min
High point	Punta della Croce (2478m/8130ft)
Maps	IGC 107 Monte Bianco Courmayeur 1:25,000, Rando Editions A1 Pays du Mont Blanc 1:50,000
Public transport	Bus or train to Morgex, bus to Arpy
Season	June to September

This trail provides stupendous views of the whole south side of the Mont Blanc massif, and the ruined fortifications on the summit of Punta della Croce are stunning. You're unlikely to see any other nationality than Italians here, so there's a real sense of having escaped the honeypot tourist areas.

Safety

Don't be tempted to run this route if there's any remaining snow in the gully below the Arpy lake, as there's significant avalanche risk throughout the winter months in this region. See the Arpy webcam at www.lovevda.it/en/before-your-trip/webcams and look for any snow in big gully on left of image.

---

1 There are two parallel trails ascending the valley from the hamlet of Arpy – one on each side of the stream. Follow either path up the clearing in the obvious valley ahead of you. The paths converge at 1748m, where the trail ascends more steeply with the river to its R. Soon after the trees thin out, cross a footbridge onto the far bank and follow the path upwards to reach the Arpy lake.

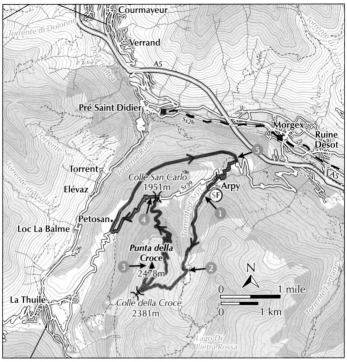

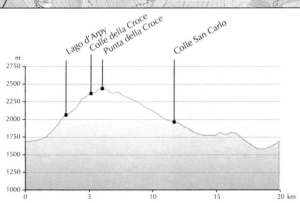

On the summit of Punta della Croce

2 Cut around the R side of the lake, and the path leads upwards to the R to **Colle della Croce** (Col de la Croix) at 2381m. There's just over 300m of ascent, so pace your running well. As you arrive at the pass you can see the village of La Thuile far below. Turn R and follow the ridgeline upwards, past a radio transmitter and wooden cross, and onwards to a stone wall. Follow the wall line beyond to reach the wonderfully located ruined fort on **Punta della Croce** (2478m).

3 After taking in the views, return to the pass and look for a higher traverse past a ruined building, leading off in a NE direction. Run along this, traversing under the summit slopes of Punta della Croce, and after one zig-zag arrive at a path junction at just under 2200m. Ignore the path joining from the L, and descend the series of bends ahead. Drop into the treeline, and the trail winds its way through the forest to join another trail before heading onwards to arrive at the **Colle San Carlo** (1951m).

Slow down on difficult ground

There are lots of loose rocks on the summit ridge, and especially around the ruins of the fortifications. Don't feel that you have to run every step; take your time, as the final section is quite airy.

View down from the summit ruins

4. Turn L and run along the road. Cross the pass and descend on the far side. At 1800m, look out for a track on the RH side leading towards buildings at **Petosan**. Continue along the trail, ignoring the L turnoff down the hill next to a building after 2km. Keep traversing around the Tête d'Arpy, and enjoy a long descending run that loops right around the mountain.

5. Ignore another LH turn after a further 1.5km and keep veering R to arrive at the road below Arpy at 1600m. Turn R and follow the road upwards on a series of bends to arrive back in **Arpy** village.

The UTMB finish line near Chamonix church (Route 37)

INTERNATIONAL RACE RECCES

Route 37
Ultra Trail du Mont Blanc (UTMB)

Start/Finish	Town hall, Chamonix (1035m/3395ft)
Distance	168km (104½ miles)
Ascent/Descent	9618m (31,555ft)
Grade	Trail running, Level 2 (with 30km of Level 3)
Time	40hrs
High point	Grand Col Ferret (2525m/8284ft)
Maps	IGN 3531 St Gervais 1:25,000, IGN 3630 Chamonix 1:25,000, IGC 107 Monte Bianco Courmayeur 1:25,000, Rando Editions A1 Pays du Mont Blanc 1:50,000
Public transport	Bus/train to Chamonix
Season	July to September
Note	Carry your passport in case you need to return across a road border, such as taking the bus from Courmayeur or Champex to Chamonix. Your insurance documents are also essential, as mountain rescue in Italy and Switzerland is not free. Carry enough cash for food, as huts often don't accept bank cards.

Running the full trail around Mont Blanc is a goal for thousands of runners each year – either as part of the Ultra Trail du Mont Blanc (UTMB) race or for personal enjoyment and a challenge. You'll pass hundreds of trekkers carrying large rucksacks as they hike the Tour du Mont Blanc, and they may think you crazy for running it fast and light.

This circuit takes in three countries – France, Italy and Switzerland – and involves a total ascent of well over the height of Everest from sea level. It's a mammoth undertaking in one push, but it can easily be split into four days of marathon-distance running for those wanting to only run in daylight or as a reconnaissance for the race. The following description therefore covers the route in four stages, each ending at a major settlement where facilities are plentiful. Suggestions for overnight accommodation are CAF Les Contamines at the end of Stage 1 (http://chaletdescontamines. ffcam.fr or tel +33 (0)450 470 088); Hotel Dolonne at the end of Stage 2 (www.hoteldolonne.com or tel +39 0165 846 674); and Chalet Club Alpin

Suisse at the end of Stage 3 (www.auclubalpin or tel +41 (0)277 831 161). See Appendix A for more contact details for sourcing accommodation on or near the route.

Whatever speed you run this route, to finish it is one of life's great achievements. The UTMB race attracts runners from around 80 different countries, which demonstrates the route's fame and magnitude.

Safety

This route is over four marathons long, plus nearly 10,000m in height gain. Only undertake it if you're properly prepared. Remember that only about half of those who set off to run this as a single push reach the finish. Listen to what your body is telling you, and don't be afraid to stop if you need to.

Stage 1 – Chamonix to Les Contamines
31km (19¼ miles), 1485m (4875ft) ascent, 1370m (4490ft) descent, 7hr 45min

1. Start in front of Chamonix town hall, and leaving the church behind you, run into the square and turn R along Rue Paccard. Keep running straight down the pedestrian street and along the road out of town. When you reach the climbing crag at Les Gaillands, veer R onto a bridleway path that follows the river all the way to Les Houches. Just before you arrive at the SNCF station, turn L across the flyover bridge above the highway, and on the far side at the road T-junction, turn R and run along the road into central **Les Houches**.

2. Just after passing the Bellevue cable car, look for Tour du Mont Blanc (TMB) signs on the L and follow these up the zig-zags of a forest track, and then a road, to reach the Maison Neuve ski lift. Here head R and follow signs for the Col de Voza. The trail ascends steeply through the trees. Just before you

---

The UTMB as a training route

If running this route for yourself and not as part of the actual UTMB race, you'll need to plan ahead for where you can get food and drinks. Mountain huts will all sell you a hot meal and refreshments, and all the villages you run through have shops. Don't set off thinking you have to carry everything completely unsupported.

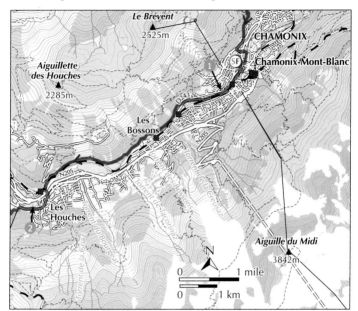

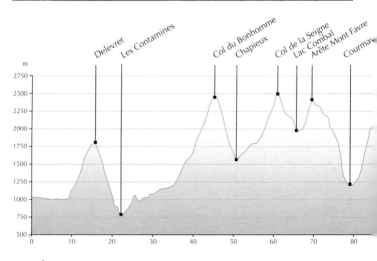

Approaching the Col du Bonhomme

reach the **pass**, take the track on the R up to Le Delevret and past the farm buildings at La Charme. You're now at the high point of this stage, before the long descent to St Gervais. Away to your L are great views up to the Col du Bonhomme.

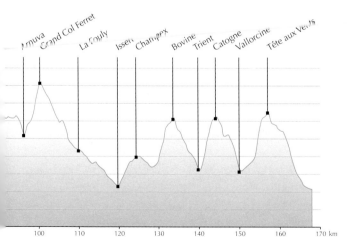

3 As you pass under the chairlift cables, turn off L and run down the ski piste, and then trails, to cross the Tramway du Mont Blanc railway lines just before the hamlet of **Montivon**. Here turn R and follow the track downwards to Le Vernay. Just after these buildings, before a sharp L corner, take a R turn and cross the stream.

Turn L at the road on the far side and take the steep descent straight down into **St Gervais**. Follow the one-way system into the town square and then pass the church, and at the roundabout where the road turns L to Les Contamines, take the R exit which leads down towards a bridge.

4 Just before the bridge, turn L into a car park and onto a trail. This track is called the Promenade du Mont Blanc, and it soon reaches **Les Praz**, where you cross the river bridge to continue the trail on the far bank. Continue until the power lines ahead indicate you've arrived at the electricity station, and cut R up the zig-zags into the forest on a short, steep ascent.

5 At a path junction turn L up the valley, and at the next split, cut L down towards the bridge and the rubbish tip. Follow the road up towards Veroce, then run the trails through **Le Ouy** and **Les Meuniers**. Here pick up the roads until you cross the main river close to a sawmill. On the far bank, turn immediately R and run along the river path until it brings you into **Les Contamines**.

Stage 2 – Les Contamines to Courmayeur
48km (30 miles), 3035m (9955ft) ascent, 2990m (9815ft) descent, 11hr 15min

6 This is a mountain stage, and the navigation is far easier than on the first stage as there's generally only one path to follow, so you can concentrate on the running. Head along the road up the valley out of **Les Contamines**, and at the roundabout next to the bridge, cross the footbridge on the R. Run up the river trails to **Le Lay** and veer L into the Nordic skiing area. Follow the trails from here until you reach the church of **Notre Dame de la Gorge**.

7 On the E bank of the bridge, the trail starts a steep climb up bare rock; follow this trail all the way up the valley over the Roman Bridge, past the **Refuge du Nant Borrant** and up to the **Refuge La Balme**. Here the wide trail turns into single track trails as you start the long ascent to the Col de Bonhomme. After cutting under power lines, pass the Tumulus and the rocky Plan des Dames before the trail steepens and then rounds off to reach the **col** at 2329m.

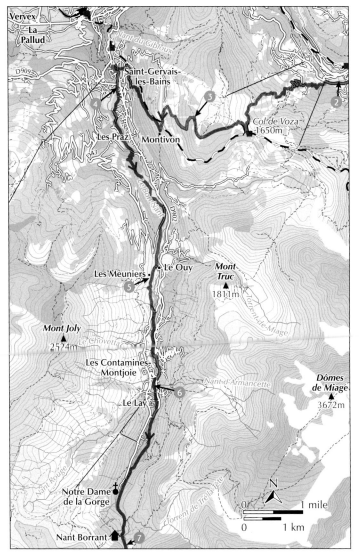

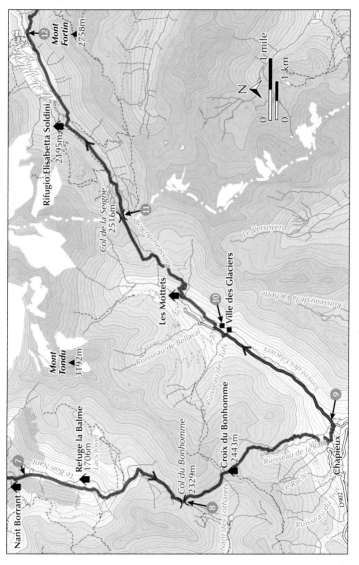

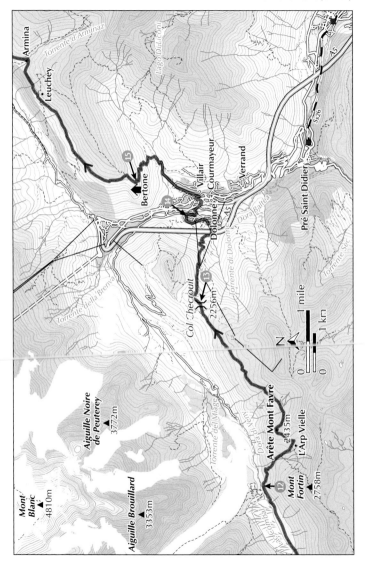

Passing Lac Combal in Val Veni

8 Head L, and the route crosses rocky steps as it traverses steeper ground. Look for dots of paint on the rocks to stay on the trail. Your next objective is the **Refuge du Col de la Croix du Bonhomme**, but you won't see this until you pass the cairn at 2479m and it's a few hundred metres below you. The descent to the hamlet of Les Chapieux is nearly 1000m on technical single track, so be wary of the ground underfoot, and of pushing too hard and exhausting the quads.

9 At **Les Chapieux**, follow the road L up the valley until you reach the **Ville des Glaciers farm**. (After the long descent, it's often hard to get back into a good running rhythm on this road section.)

10 Cross the bridge and follow the track up towards the refuge at **Les Mottets**. Just after crossing a footbridge before the hut, turn R up the hillside on a series of steep switchbacks. These ease off above 2100m, before a more exposed traverse across a stream, then there's a long steady incline to reach the Italian border at **Col de la Seigne** (2516m).

(11) The descent on the far side is soft underfoot and you can run fast towards the valley floor, where you pick up a jeep track. Just before reaching the end of the hanging valley opposite the Elisabetta Soldini hut, cross to the R of the stream and follow the single track down to the Val Veni. Join the long straight of the main track leading to **Lac Combal** and the huge moraine wall of the Miage glacier, which blocks the valley.

(12) Before you reach the bridge after Lac Combal, look for a track on the R that heads up the hillside to **L'Arp Vielle**. Run through the old farm ruins and to the upper alpage farm at 2303m. Here, curve around L on a rising traverse to cross the **Arête Mont Favre**. Just after, a short steep descent is followed by a lovely rolling run into the Courmayeur ski area. Follow the yellow paint markings of the TMB until you reach the Refuge Maison Vielle at **Col Checrouit** (2256m).

(13) Run down the track towards the Plan Checrouit cable car and look out for the start of a small single track on the L, which descends beneath the cables. It zig-zags down through the forest and brings you out at the top of the nursery ski slopes at **Dolonne**. Follow the TMB signs through the old cobbled streets, and when you reach the road, follow it across the bridge and up on the far side to reach the main square of **Courmayeur** and the bus station.

Stage 3 – Courmayeur to Champex
45km (28 miles), 2660m (8720ft) ascent, 2390m (7835ft) descent, 10hr 15min

(14) Directly behind **Courmayeur** bus station is a steep road leading up into the town. Follow this, and the TMB signs, to run along the road through the village of **Villair**. The road turns into a forest track; run along this to a bridge on your L. Cross the bridge, and on the far side the trail suddenly ascends the hillside in what feels like a never-ending series of zig-zags up a well-maintained stone track. As you leave the treeline behind, the **Bertone hut** is soon reached and refreshments are available.

(15) Continue ahead to a viewing table just beyond the hut, then ignore a track cutting up R to the Mont de la Saxe and run ahead on the balcony trail around to **Leuchey**. Just above these buildings, the TMB track cuts R across the hillside to La Leche, then after a stream-crossing reaches **Armina**. Continue through Sécheron, and one kilometre later turn R at a path junction to run up to the beautiful **Bonatti hut**.

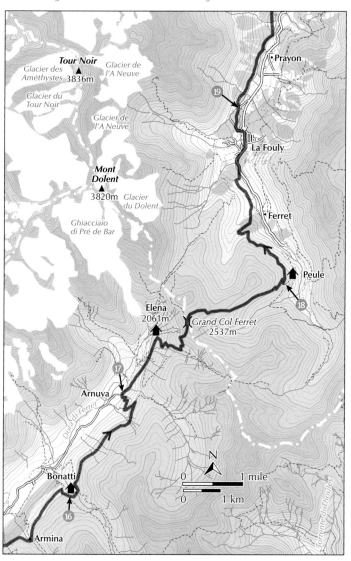

On the traverse between the Bertone and Bonatti huts

16 The view from the terrace of Bonatti is unparalleled, so it's well worth stopping for a bite to eat, and to take in the vistas back along the Italian Val Ferret to Mont Blanc and the Col de la Seigne. The path behind the hut splits at some ruined buildings, where you turn L to cross a stream. On the far side there's a rising traverse from the farm buildings; follow this for several kilometres until you're above the village of **Arnuva**, which the trail descends steeply to reach.

17 Run up the valley, and on the far side of a stream crossing, turn R towards Sagioan (1933m), on the smaller RH path. This leads up to the main track above the **Elena refuge**, where you turn R up the zig-zags that climb the hillside. This is a long climb, quite muddy in places, eventually leading to the **Grand Col Ferret** (2537m) – the highest point on the route. The descent on the far side into Switzerland is easy to run, and you can enjoy a fast pace to the **Peule hut**.

18 Don't descend the TMB route, but look for the small trail cutting across the hillside over the Ravine de la Peule and onwards to Le Plampro (1925m).

This tiny trail is really wild and rarely used, except by runners on a UTMB reconnaissance, and Plampro is the start of your descent into the Swiss Val Ferret. Rejoin the TMB track after the village of **Ferret**, and turn L to follow it down the valley to **La Fouly**.

(19) Continue along the TMB trails alongside the river, running past the villages of **Prayon** and then Branche on the opposite bank. Take a small trail on the L and run to the old lateral moraine of the **Saleina glacier**, and when you reach it turn R to run down the Crête de Saleina. Rejoin the TMB track at the bridge at 1207m and turn L to run through **Praz de Fort**. The old wooden buildings with their rat stones are exceptionally well preserved and pretty.

(20) Cross the main road and follow the TMB trail to Issert, where you run along the main road for a short while before turning off L to climb again. This is the start of the Sentier des Champignons, which ascends through the forests to Champex. Keep following the TMB signs, which brings you to a small road. Turn L and follow it into **Champex**, where there are plenty of shops and cafés to replenish your stocks.

Stage 4 – Champex to Chamonix
46km (28½ miles), 2710m (8895ft) ascent, 3140m (10,305ft) descent, 10hr 45min

(21) The final stage of the route is nicely varied, with just three major ascents: Bovine, Catogne and Tête aux Vents. Start by running NE along the lake and up the main street of **Champex**. At the far end the road ascends slightly, and you pass the Breya chair lift on your L. Almost immediately afterwards, bear L onto a forest track past Gîte Bon Abri and run onwards until just before the village of **La Poya**, at Plan de l'Au, where you turn sharp L up the hillside towards the Bovine alpage. You're following the TMB, so the route is well marked.

(22) Traverse upwards to the stream crossings at **La Jure** before zig-zagging up to climb well above the treeline. When the trail heads R, you're on the contour around to the farm building at **Bovine**, where refreshments are available. On a clear day there are great views down to Martigny and along the Rhone valley.

(23) Continue up to the high point at **Portalo** before running a great descent down into the trees past **La Giète** in its alpage, and onwards to the **Col de la Forclaz** (1527m). Keep L of the road at the col, and head along the trail up

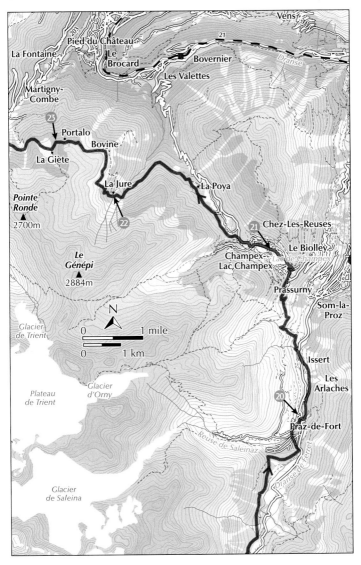

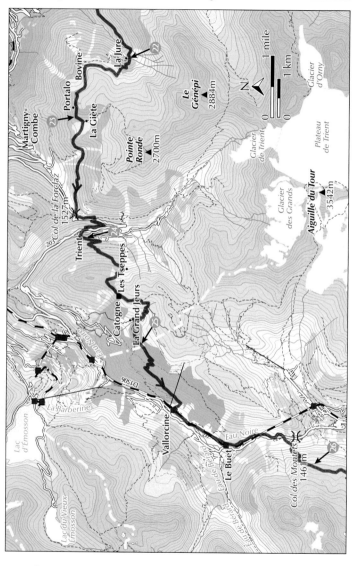

the valley for a short while before turning R down the steep path directly to **Trient**, crossing the road twice.

24 Cut around the church to the R, and against the hillside is a forestry track cutting upwards to the L. Take this and follow signs for Les Tseppes, which is just above the treeline again. Here the trail curves around the hillside to bring you to **Catogne**, which marks the start of a long, steep descent along the Nant de Catogne stream, on its R bank. As you near the treeline, the route cuts L towards **La Grand Jeurs**, where you leave Switzerland and enter France again.

25 Run onwards to Les Saix Blancs and follow the signs down to **Vallorcine**. At the train station, cross the railway tracks and turn L and up the valley on the river trail, past **Le Buet** and onwards up to the **Col des Montets** (1461m). This is a long, steady ascent, and it's essential to recover on it before the last major climb ahead. At the col, turn R to cross the road to the visitor centre and head L along the trail. Ignore the two L turns and keep running up the hill.

Runners gather at the start line of in Chamonix on race day

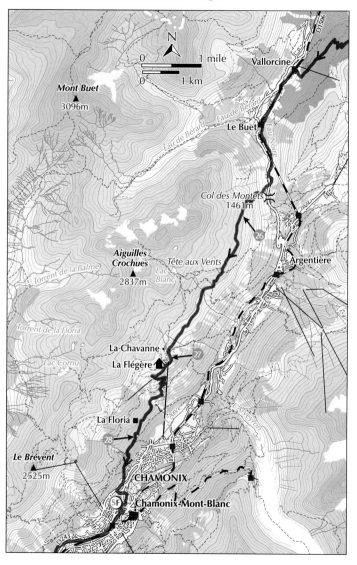

26 The track ascends steeply towards a cliff line and traverses L beneath it. There are a couple of sections with steps, then after you pass a small cairn on your L the angle slackens off and you make a long, steady traverse up to reach the **Tête aux Vents** (2132m). Ahead is a breathtaking view of Mont Blanc. At the large cairn, cross the path ascending from Aiguillette d'Argentière to **Lac Blanc** and continue onwards to Chalet des Chéserys over a very rocky section. This trail leads onwards across the Aiguilles Rouges to reach **La Chavanne**.

27 Run towards the **Flégère** cable car and pass it to the L to pick up the ski piste below. Continue along this until you reach a wide L turn in a bowl, and take the sharp L turnoff onto a single track down through the forest. This descends under the téléphérique cables for a while before veering R.

Cross a jeep track and continue on the small trail on the far side, following signs for La Floria. There are a few turnoffs, but ignore them and continue to the buvette at **La Floria**. Here is a last chance for refreshments before the final descent into Chamonix, which you can see below.

28 Below La Floria the trail widens, and it brings you out into the Les Nants area of **Chamonix**. When you reach the road, head R along it and continue to a mini-roundabout. Turn L here and run down to the main road; turn L and then R down Avenue de la Plage. After crossing the river, turn R onto the promenade and run past the sports halls and school, then at the next bridge turn R past the Alpine hotel and immediately L down the pedestrian high street.

At the clock tower turn L, then at the statue of Dr Paccard turn R and follow the river into the square. At the statues of de Saussure and Balmat, turn R past the post office and run up to the finish in front of the town hall.

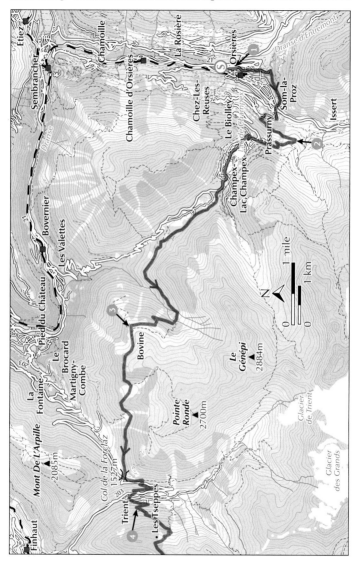

Route 38
Orsières, Champex, Chamonix (OCC)

Start	Main church, Orsières (911m/2988ft)
Finish	Town hall, Chamonix (1035m/3395ft)
Distance	53km (33 miles)
Ascent	3300m (10,825ft)
Descent	3176m (10,420ft)
Grade	Trail running, Level 2
Time	10hr 30min
High point	Catogne (2040m/6693ft)
Maps	IGN 3630 Chamonix 1:25,000, Swiss Topo 1345 Orsières 1:25,000, Rando Editions A1 Pays du Mont Blanc 1:50,000
Public transport	Train to Martigny, then bus to Orsières
Season	June to September

This is the 'little sister' of the Ultra Trail du Mont Blanc. The route starts in Orsières below Champex and follows the final section of the UTMB (Route 37), with a few minor alternations to make it more accessible and faster to run.

The village of Trient is an ideal place to split the trail if you choose to run the race route over two days. The Auberge du Mont Blanc is well situated and reasonably priced (www.aubergemontblanc.com/en or tel +41 (0)277 671 505).

Safety

After very heavy rain the stream at La Jure is dangerous to cross, so only run this route in a period of stable weather.

Stage 1 – Orsières to Trient
22km (13¾ miles), 1495m (4900ft) ascent, 1100m (3615ft) descent, 4hr 45min

1 From the church on Rue de l'Eglise, run down the narrow Rue de la Commune and follow the small road S on the E bank of the river until it turns

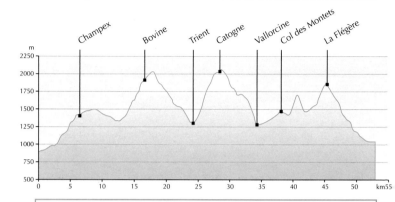

> ## Keeping cool
>
> This route rarely goes above the treeline, so the air is often hot and there's little breeze – dress in light clothing to keep cool. You'll pass many water troughs where you can refill your water bottle – look out for signs saying *eau potable* to ensure that the water is drinkable.

into a trail, which leads to the La Borratay bridge. On the far side turn R and run upstream to reach the next bridge at **Som la Proz**. Cross it, and when you reach the road turn L, then go R at the T-junction.

After 100m, cut off L onto a trail and run uphill to the footbridge, where you turn R onto the contour track, following signs for Prassurny. Stay on the upward trail and soon reach the Sentier des Champignons. Here you join the main UTMB trail, which is described in full in Route 37. Note, however, that there are two minor variations: the first between Prassurny and Bovine, and the second between Col des Montets and La Flégère. A brief onward description is therefore given here, incorporating these variations.

2 Follow the Sentier de Champignons all the way up the hillside and into **Champex**. Run alongside the lake and out of town past the Breya lift, and onto the forest track towards La Poya. At Plan de l'Au, veer L and upwards into the La Jure valley. At a stream crossing, cut R and take the lower track to **Bovine**, where you meet the main UTMB route again.

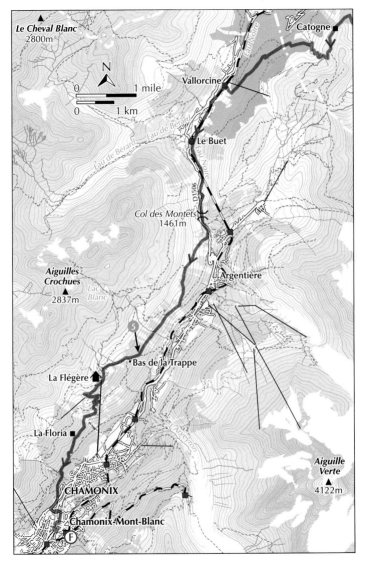

(3) Run through the Bovine alpage, overlooking the Rhone valley and Martigny down to your R. At the end of the alpage, start descending towards the **Col de Forclaz** and then down the trails into the village of **Trient**.

Stage 2 – Trient to Chamonix
31km (19¼ miles), 1830m (6000ft) ascent, 2100m (6885ft) descent, 5hr 45min

(4) From Trient, ascend towards Catogne past the farm at **Les Tseppes**, and soon after, run down the trails towards **Vallorcine** and onwards up the river track to reach the **Col des Montets**. Here, ignore the UTMB track cutting up R to the Tête aux Vents, and follow the trail ahead until you see a path on the R signposted to the Aiguillette d'Argentière. Run up this to path junction at the treeline, then turn L and descend to a path junction at 1437m, where you take a long rising traverse to the **Bas de la Trappe**.

(5) At a junction at 1579m, turn R up the hill on a series of zig-zags and follow the signs to **La Flégère**. You emerge out of the trees into the ski area, and once past the Flégère cable car station and mountain hut you rejoin the UTMB route once again. Having turned off the

Running in the Aiguilles Rouges

ski piste, descend quickly, passing the Chalet de Floria, before emerging into the Les Nants area of **Chamonix**.

Turn L at the Clos de Savoy roundabout, then L again on the main road, before taking an almost immediate R down Avenue de la Plage. As soon as you run over the river bridge, turn R, and at the next bridge turn R again before taking a L down the pedestrian street into the main town square. The race finish loops past the statues of Balmat and Saussure before the crossing the line in front of the town hall.

Route 39
Courmayeur, Champex, Chamonix (CCC)

Start	Place Brocherel, Courmayeur (1210m/3969ft)
Finish	Town hall, Chamonix (1035m/3395ft)
Distance	101km (62¾ miles)
Ascent	6745m (22,130ft)
Descent	6570m (21,555ft)
Grade	Trail running, Level 2 (with 2km of Level 3)
Time	22hrs
High point	Tête de la Tronche (2584m/8477ft)
Maps	IGN 3630 Chamonix 1:25,000, IGC 107 Monte Bianco Courmayeur 1:25,000, Rando Editions A1 Pays du Mont Blanc 1:50,000
Public transport	Bus to Courmayeur
Season	July to September

This is effectively the half-UTMB route, starting at Courmayeur, with a route variation to the Bertone refuge. It's very runnable, with the greatest technical difficulties on the Tête de la Tronche – the highest point of the run.

This route could be split into three stages, the logical overnight breaks being at La Fouly (try Auberge des Glaciers: www.aubergedesglaciers.ch or tel +41 (0)277 831 171) and at Trient (Auberge Mont Blanc: www.aubergemont blanc.com/en or tel +41 (0)277 671 505), creating daily distances of 36km (22½ miles), 30km (18½ miles) and 35km (21¾ miles).

Safety

Ensure that your phone allows international roaming, as you run from Italy into Switzerland and then France on this route. Emergency service numbers are different in each country: in Italy it's 118, in Switzerland 144, and in France 112. If you're undertaking this route in one go and therefore running almost a whole night, take a spare headtorch as well as fresh batteries for your primary headtorch, to ensure there'll be no problem lighting your way.

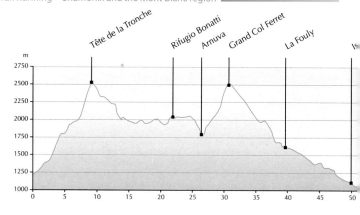

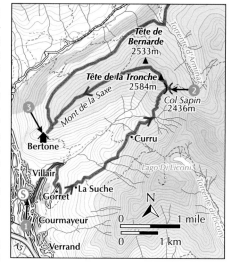

1. From Place Brocherel in Courmayeur, follow the UTMB (Route 37) to **Villair**, where you turn off R to ascend to **Gorret**, and then onwards via trails to the hamlet of **La Suche**. After this steep ascent the route traverses the increasingly steep hillside to **Curru**, and then up zig-zags to the **Col Sapin** (2436m).

2. Turn L here to ascend the rubble-strewn path to **Tête de la Tronche**. The ridge is a little exposed, so take extra care. Traverse below the **Tête de Bernarde**, on its southern slopes, to reach the broad shoulder of **Mont de la Saxe**. Follow the ridge to its end, where it drops steeply to reach the **Bertone hut**. You can get refreshments here.

220

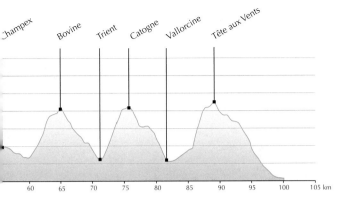

3 From Bertone, follow Route 37 (from waypoint 15) to **Champex** and then all the way to the finish point in **Chamonix**.

Using poles

Poles are highly recommended for running this route to provide extra balance on rough ground – especially upwards from Col Sapin. If you're prone to blisters, wear gloves to protect your hands from rubbing on the poles.

Crossing the Tête aux Vents boulders between the Col des Montets and La Flégère

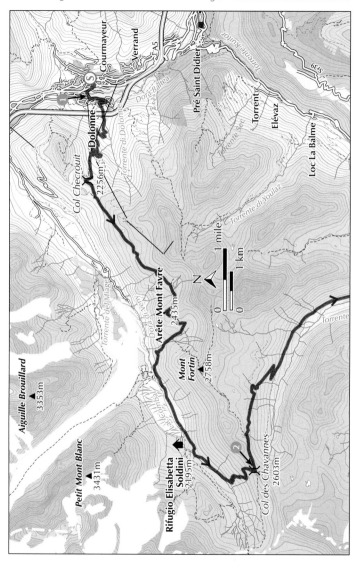

Route 40
Traces des Ducs de Savoie (TDS)

Start	Bus station, Courmayeur (1210m/3969ft)
Finish	Town hall, Chamonix (1035m/3395ft)
Distance	119km (74 miles)
Ascent	7250m (23,785ft)
Descent	7075m (23,215ft)
Grade	Trail running, Level 3 (with 5km of Level 4)
Time	27hr 30min
High point	Col des Chavannes (2603m/8540ft)
Maps	IGN 3531 St Gervais, 3532 Les Arcs, 3532 Beaufortain, 3531 Megève (all 1:25,000); Rando Editions A1 Pays du Mont Blanc and A2 Beaufortain (1:50,000)
Public transport	Bus to Courmayeur, and from Chamonix
Season	July to September

As its name suggests, this route explores the former Savoie state, which united regions of the Italian Aosta valley and the Tarentaise, Beaufort and Contamines valleys of the French Savoie before their respective countries annexed them. The trail includes several passages above 2500m, and is technical and exposed in several places, as well as having long remote and committing sections.

If you wish to split this route over several days, the most obvious splits are at Col du Petit Saint Bernard (Gîte du Petit Saint Bernard: tel +33 (0)662 191 976) and Les Contamines (try Refuge Nant Borrant: www.refuge-nantborrant.com or tel +33 (0)450 470 357). The route directly passes both of these accommodation options. Note that the second of the three stages is significantly longer that the others.

Stage 1 – Courmayeur to Col du Petit Saint Bernard
37km (21¾ miles), 2600m (8535ft) ascent, 1635m (5360ft) descent, 8hr 45min

1 From Courmayeur bus station, run under the main road underpass to cross the river into **Dolonne**, and follow the road up L to the nursery ski slopes before following the ski piste up the hillside to **Col Checrouit** (2256m).

> ### Safety
>
> There are few sections of commercial trail running race routes more exposed than the descent from the Passeur de Pralognan (2567m). It's a good idea to carry a short walkers' confidence rope in case a fixed rope is not in place – especially in wet weather. Get advice on conditions before you start out, and don't consider this route in snowy conditions.

From here, run along the UTMB (Route 37) in reverse via **Arête Mont Favre** to **Lac Combal**, and just after passing the **Elisabetta Soldini hut**, cut L and start ascending steeply to **Col des Chavannes** (2603m). This is the highest pass on the route, and the descent on the far side is gentle and fast to run.

2 Follow the Vallon des Chavannes all the way down to **Alpetta**, then drop off R below the track to cross a bridge and climb up R on the far side. At a corner of the road next to the trail, veer R and follow the track until it crosses the Doire stream, before turning L to ascend slowly to **Lago di Verney**. As you reach the lake, keep to the R of it and run to the far side, where there's a brutally steep but short ascent to the **Col du Petit Saint Bernard** (2188m).

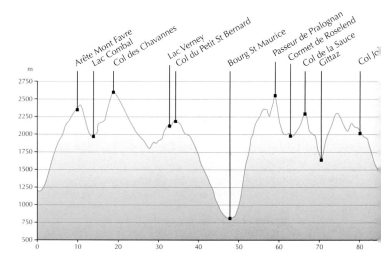

Stage 2 – Col du Petit Saint Bernard to Les Contamines
52km (32½ miles), 3290m (10,795ft) ascent, 4310m (14,135ft) descent, 12hrs

3 Here you leave Italy and enter France, embarking on the very long descent into Bourg Saint Maurice. Run past the old hospice, and on the corner of the road beyond, turn R and follow the track across the river, and then onwards along the valley side. At a path junction at 1982m, just after passing under the electric pylons, take the RH track – the Tour de la Haute Tarentaise trail. Follow this for several kilometres to reach **St Germain**.

4 Run past a water mill, following signs for Séez. These lead you onto forest trails, and eventually a track and then road into town. Turn L past the town hall and pass the electricity station on the far side. Cross the road to the R, and once you've crossed the river, turn L into the sports fields and parks area. On their far side is the main **Bourg St Maurice** train station and the town square. Run along the pedestrian street until you pass the church, and turn R up the streets ascending the hillside.

5 Signs to Fort du Truc lead you through **La Rosière** and **Le Replatet**, and upwards to the village of Le Grand Replat where you turn L to climb to the ruins of a fort. Run past it to the R, then curve L to ascend again to **Fort de la Platte**. This climb up from Bourg St Maurice is huge, so take on plenty of water and pace yourself well.

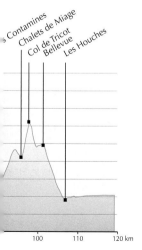

6 Beyond the fort, follow signs for Col de Forclaz and **Les Cinq Lacs**. After the pass you soon reach the first lake (Lac Esola), and next to the spot height of 2333m take the RH path, which descends steeply to the **Chalet de la Combe**. Turn R at the ruins and run upwards to the 2400m contour, where the route turns sharp R to traverse the steep hillside. Be very wary of loose rocks here.

7 After traversing, veer N to reach the Passeur de Pralognan (2567m). On the far side is the most technical section of the entire route, as you descend to the trail head at 1999m. Take the initial descent extremely carefully, and

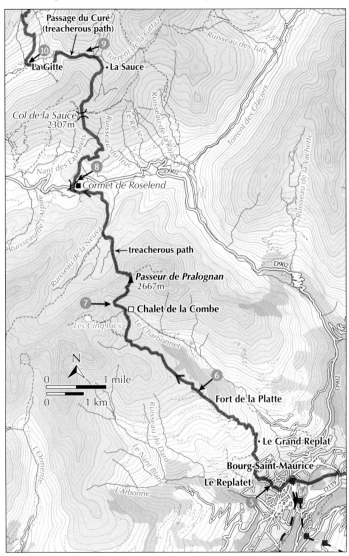

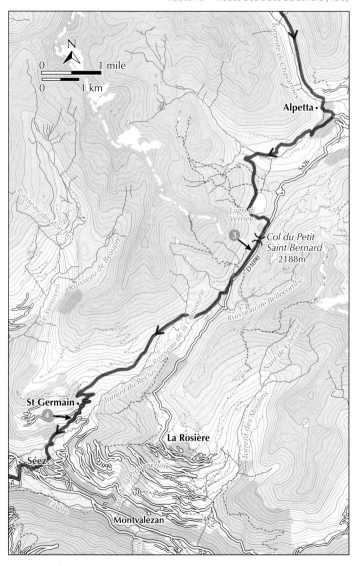

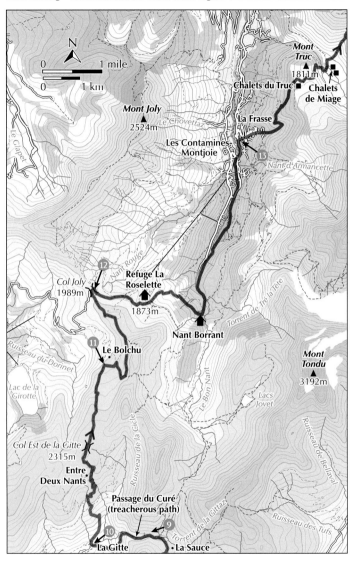

use the bolts and any fixed ropes in situ. Once on the road, run N to reach the **Cormet de Roselend**, where you can stop for refreshments.

8 Cross the road and turn R, then go almost immediately L on a small track. This eventually gives way to a very marshy ascent on a rising traverse to the Col de la Sauce (2307m). The descent on the far side is initially gentle, and then steep and erosion-rutted. Reach the buildings at **La Sauce** and follow the Gittaz river down on an incredible section of trail.

9 Enter a gorge where the path is hewn out of the rock on the L bank of the river, with a fearsome drop-off to your R. This is the infamous Passage du Curé, the steepest section of which is inset into an almost perpendicular cliff. Three miners lost their lives in the construction of this amazing section of trail, and their ghosts are said to haunt the trail at night.

10 The trail soon widens and eases off to reach the hamlet of **La Gitte**, where you turn upwards once again, past La Laichere to a path junction at 1857m. Here turn L to a track junction at 1968m. Take the RH jeep track, heading in a NE direction, and at the next junction turn L and continue to **Entre Deux Nants**. Keep the stream on your L and follow an increasingly indistinct path up to the **Col Est de la Gitte**, then head N into La Grande Pierrière.

11 Run along the trail towards **Le Bolchu**, but head R towards the lakes at 2000m and zig-zag upwards to gain the Tour du Pays du Mont Blanc trail, which you follow over rocky ground N to the Tête du Lac de Roselette and onwards to **Col du Joly** (1989m).

12 Turn R and run along the ski piste, past the lake and mountain hut of **La Roselette**, then past Bûche Croisée and La Chenalattaz, to reach the **Nant Borrant hut** on steeper forest trails. Here you pick up the UTMB (Route 37), and follow it in reverse to **Les Contamines** down the valley.

Stage 3 – Les Contamines to Chamonix
30km (18¾ miles), 1445m (4745ft) ascent, 1580m (5190ft) descent, 6hr 45min

13 From the centre of Les Contamines, turn R at the church and run up the cut-throughs to **La Frasse**, where the road gives way to a large forest track. Follow this upwards towards the **Chalets du Truc**, which are well sign-posted. Just before reaching the chalets you emerge above the treeline; pass the building to the R, now heading to the Chalets de Miage. On the

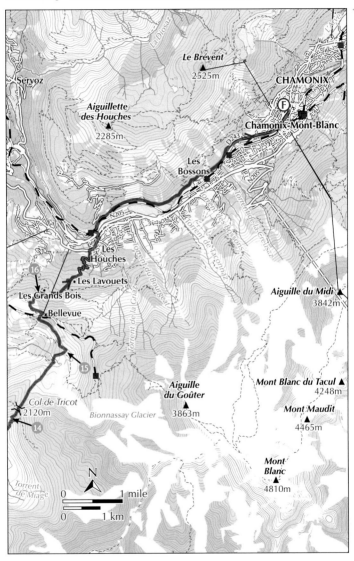

Servoz

Le Brévent
2525m

CHAMONIX

Aiguillette
des Houches
2285m

Chamonix-Mont-Blanc

Les
Bossons

Les
Houches

16

Les Lavouets

Les Grands Bois

Bellevue

15

Aiguille du Midi
3842m

Mont Blanc du Tacul ▲
4248m

Col de Tricot
2120m

14

Bionnassay Glacier

Aiguille
du Goûter

3863m

Mont Maudit
▲
4465m

Mont
Blanc
▲
4810m

Torrent
de Miage

N

0   1 mile

0   1 km

Shoes and running repairs

Wear more technical grippy trail shoes than normal for this route, as you'll encounter loose rock, mud and steep trails. Sometimes a shoe sole may become partially detached during a run over rough ground – take a 1m length of gaffer tape wrapped around a walking pole; in an emergency you can use it to strap your shoes together as a temporary repair.

---

far side of the Truc plateau is a steep single-track descent to **Miage**, and beyond it the zig-zags ascending to Col de Tricot are obvious.

14 The ascent to **Col de Tricot** (2120m) is very steep and hard to run. It's also quite exposed near the top, so take extra care. On the far side there's a wonderful descent down eroded trails towards a gorge at the base of the **Bionnassay glacier**. As you reach it, ignore the trail joining from the L, and descend R. This brings you to a Himalayan-style cable suspension bridge over the river. Don't run on the bridge, and only have a maximum of two people on it at a time.

15 On the far side, climb upwards to reach the main trail, then turn L and follow signs for Bellevue. There are a few exposed sections, protected with cables and steps. As you reach **Bellevue**, cross the Tramway du Mont Blanc tracks and run to the cable car station. Descend steeply beyond the cable car, along the alpage in the direction of Chalet de Praz Dru, then turn R and run to the bottom of the Téléski, where the track drops down R into the forest.

16 At **Les Grands Bois**, turn R and run the steep singletrack underneath the Bellevue cable car lines to the road head at **Les Lavouets**. Run down the road, ignoring any turnoffs, until you reach the main road. Turn R into the centre of **Les Houches**, where again you meet the UTMB (Route 37) and follow it in reverse along the river track all the way into **Chamonix** to finish in front of the town hall.

Appendix A
Useful contacts

Tourist information

France
Chamonix
www.chamonix.com

Les Contamines
www.en.lescontamines.com

Bourg St Maurice
www.bourgsaintmaurice.fr

Vallorcine
www.vallorcine.com

Italy
Courmayeur
www.lovevda.it

Switzerland
Saint Bernard
www.saint-bernard.ch

Champex
www.champex.ch

Trient
www.trient.ch

Accommodation
www.hostelworld.com
www.booking.com
www.hotelf1.com

Chamonix
Chamonix youth hostel
www.auberge-chamonix.com

Gîte Alpenrose
www.chamonix-alpenrose.com

Chamonix Lodge
chamonixlodge.com

Moëde Anterne hut
www.refuge-moede-anterne.com

Les Contamines
CAF Les Contamines
chaletdescontamines.ffcam.fr

Refuge Nant Borrant
www.refuge-nantborrant.com

Col du Petit Saint Bernard
Gîte du Petit Saint Bernard
www.bureau-montagne-haute-tarentaise.fr

Courmayeur
Hotel Dolonne
www.hoteldolonne.com

Rifugio Bonatti
www.rifugiobonatti.it

Champex

Chalet Club Alpin Suisse
www.auclubalpin.ch

Gîte Bon Abri
www.gite-bon-abri.com

Trient
Trient Auberge du Mont Blanc
www.aubergemontblanc.com

Vallorcine
Gîte Mermoud
www.cvmmontblanc.fr

Refuge Loriaz
loriaz.fr

Transport

Air
Geneva airport
www.gva.ch

Skyscanner (flight-finder website)
www.skyscanner.net

Easyjet
www.easyjet.com

Airport transfer
EasyBus
www.easybus.com/en/geneva-airport

Cham-Van
www.cham-van.com/en/

Chamonix Valley Transfers
www.chamonix-valley-transfers.co.uk/

ChamExpress
www.chamexpress.com

Deluxe Transfer
www.deluxe-transfers.com

Mountain Drop-offs
www.mountaindropoffs.com

Rail
Eurostar
www.eurostar.com

Mont Blanc Express
www.mont-blanc-express.com

Mont Blanc Tramway
www.compagniedumontblanc.fr

Bus
Eurolines
www.eurolines.co.uk

SAT
www.sat-montblanc.com

SBB
www.sbb.ch/en/home

SAVDA
www.savda.it

Swiss Postbus
www.postauto.ch

Weather

France
chamonix-meteo.com
www.meteofrance.com
www.meteo-chamonix.org

Switzerland
www.meteoswiss.admin.ch
www.meteocentrale.ch

Italy
3B Meteo
www.3bmeteo.com
cf.regione.vda.it

Maps
Stanfords
www.stanfords.co.uk

The Map Shop
www.themapshop.co.uk

Icicle
www.icicle-mountaineering.ltd.uk

Emergencies and insurance

Mountain rescue
Peloton de Gendarmerie de
Haute-Montagne (PGHM)
tel +33 (0)450 531 689

Swiss mountain rescue
tel 144

Aosta mountain rescue
tel +39 0165 843 635

Emergency services
France – tel 112

Switzerland – tel 144

Italy – tel 118

Insurance providers
British Mountaineering Council
www.thebmc.co.uk/insurance

Snowcard
www.snowcard.co.uk

DogTag
www.dogtag.co.uk

Notes

download the route
in GPX Format

All the routes in this guide are available for download from:

www.cicerone.co.uk/800/GPX

as GPX files. You should be able to load them into most formats of mobile device, whether GPS or smartphone.

When you go to this link, you will be asked for your email address and where you purchased the guide, and have the option to subscribe to the Cicerone e-newsletter.

www.cicerone.co.uk

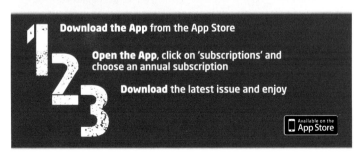

Listing of Cicerone guides

The GR5 Trail
The Robert Louis Stevenson Trail
Tour of the Oisans: The GR54
Tour of the Queyras
Tour of the Vanoise
Vanoise Ski Touring
Via Ferratas of the French Alps
Walking in Corsica
Walking in Provence – East
Walking in Provence – West
Walking in the Auvergne
Walking in the Cevennes
Walking in the Dordogne
Walking in the Haute Savoie – North & South
Walks in the Cathar Region

GERMANY

Hiking and Biking in the Black Forest
Walking in the Bavarian Alps

HIMALAYA

Annapurna
Bhutan
Everest
The Mount Kailash Trek
Trekking in Ladakh
Trekking in the Himalaya

ICELAND & GREENLAND

Trekking in Greenland
Walking and Trekking in Iceland

IRELAND

The Irish Coast to Coast Walk
The Mountains of Ireland

ITALY

Gran Paradiso
Sibillini National Park
Shorter Walks in the Dolomites
The Way of St Francis
Through the Italian Alps
Trekking in the Apennines
Trekking in the Dolomites
Via Ferratas of the Italian Dolomites: 1&2
Walking in Abruzzo
Walking in Italy's Stelvio National Park
Walking in Sardinia
Walking in Sicily
Walking in the Central Italian Alps
Walking in the Dolomites

Walking in Tuscany
Walking in Umbria
Walking on the Amalfi Coast
Walking the Italian Lakes
Walks and Treks in the Maritime Alps

MEDITERRANEAN

Jordan – Walks, Treks, Caves, Climbs and Canyons
The High Mountains of Crete
The Mountains of Greece
Treks and Climbs in Wadi Rum
Walking and Trekking on Corfu
Walking on Malta
Western Crete

NORTH AMERICA

British Columbia
The Grand Canyon
The John Muir Trail
The Pacific Crest Trail

SOUTH AMERICA

Aconcagua and the Southern Andes
Hiking and Biking Peru's Inca Trails
Torres del Paine

SCANDINAVIA

Walking in Norway

SLOVENIA, CROATIA AND MONTENEGRO

The Islands of Croatia
The Julian Alps of Slovenia
The Mountains of Montenegro
Trekking in Slovenia
Walking in Slovenia: The Karavanke

SPAIN AND PORTUGAL

Mountain Walking in Southern Catalunya
Spain's Sendero Histórico: The GR1
The Mountains of Nerja
The Northern Caminos
Trekking through Mallorca
Walking in Andalucia
Walking in Madeira
Walking in Mallorca
Walking in Menorca
Walking in the Algarve
Walking in the Cordillera Cantabrica
Walking in the Sierra Nevada

Walking on Gran Canaria
Walking on La Gomera and El Hierro
Walking on La Palma
Walking on Lanzarote and Fuerteventura
Walking on Tenerife
Walking in Costa Blanca
Walking the GR7 in Andalucia
Walks and Climbs in the Picos de Europa

SWITZERLAND

Alpine Pass Route
The Swiss Alps
Tour of the Jungfrau Region
Walking in the Bernese Oberland
Walking in the Valais
Walks in the Engadine

TECHNIQUES

Geocaching in the UK
Indoor Climbing
Lightweight Camping
Map and Compass
Mountain Weather
Outdoor Photography
Polar Exploration
Rock Climbing
Sport Climbing
The Hillwalker's Manual

MINI GUIDES

Alpine Flowers
Avalanche!
Navigating with a GPS
Navigation
Pocket First Aid and Wilderness Medicine
Snow

MOUNTAIN LITERATURE

8000 metres
A Walk in the Clouds
Abode of the Gods
Unjustifiable Risk?

For full information on all our guides, books and eBooks, visit our website:
www.cicerone.co.uk.

Walking – Trekking – Mountaineering – Climbing – Cycling

Over 40 years, Cicerone have built up an outstanding collection of over 300 guides, inspiring all sorts of amazing adventures.

 Every guide comes from extensive exploration and research by our expert authors, all with a passion for their subjects. They are frequently praised, endorsed and used by clubs, instructors and outdoor organisations.

All our titles can now be bought as **e-books**, **ePubs** and **Kindle** files and we also have an online magazine – **Cicerone Extra** – with features to help cyclists, climbers, walkers and trekkers choose their next adventure, at home or abroad.

Our website shows any **new information** we've had in since a book was published. Please do let us know if you find anything has changed, so that we can publish the latest details. On our **website** you'll also find great ideas and lots of detailed information about what's inside every guide and you can buy **individual routes** from many of them online.

It's easy to keep in touch with what's going on at Cicerone by getting our monthly **free e-newsletter**, which is full of offers, competitions, up-to-date information and topical articles. You can subscribe on our home page and also follow us on **Facebook** and **Twitter** or dip into our **blog**.

Cicerone – the very best guides for exploring the world.

CICERONE

2 Police Square Milnthorpe Cumbria LA7 7PY
Tel: 015395 62069 info@cicerone.co.uk
www.cicerone.co.uk and **www.cicerone-extra.com**